Hands-On Full Stack Development with Spring Boot 2 and React

Second Edition

Build modern and scalable full stack applications using Spring Framework 5 and React with Hooks

Juha Hinkula

BIRMINGHAM - MUMBAI

Hands-On Full Stack Development with Spring Boot 2 and React
Second Edition

Commissioning Editor: Richa Tripathi
Acquisition Editor: Shriram Shekhar
Content Development Editor: Divya Vijayan
Technical Editor: Pradeep Sahu
Copy Editor: Safis Editing
Project Coordinator: Prajakta Naik
Proofreader: Safis Editing
Indexer: Pratik Shirodkar
Graphics: Jisha Chirayil
Production Coordinator: Aparna Bhagat

First published: June 2018
Second edition: May 2019

Production reference: 1200519

Published by Packt Publishing Ltd.
Livery Place
35 Livery Street
Birmingham
B3 2PB, UK.

ISBN 978-1-83882-236-1

www.packtpub.com

To my wife, Pirre, and daughter, Anni, for their support and the time that I was able to spend with this project. To Ms. Riitta Blomster, for proofreading some difficult parts during the project. To all my motivated students, for inspiring me to continue the lifelong journey of learning.

- Juha Hinkula

`mapt.io`

Mapt is an online digital library that gives you full access to over 5,000 books and videos, as well as industry leading tools to help you plan your personal development and advance your career. For more information, please visit our website.

Why subscribe?

- Spend less time learning and more time coding with practical eBooks and Videos from over 4,000 industry professionals

- Improve your learning with Skill Plans built especially for you

- Get a free eBook or video every month

- Mapt is fully searchable

- Copy and paste, print, and bookmark content

Packt.com

Did you know that Packt offers eBook versions of every book published, with PDF and ePub files available? You can upgrade to the eBook version at `www.packt.com` and as a print book customer, you are entitled to a discount on the eBook copy. Get in touch with us at `customercare@packtpub.com` for more details.

At `www.packt.com`, you can also read a collection of free technical articles, sign up for a range of free newsletters, and receive exclusive discounts and offers on Packt books and eBooks.

Contributors

About the author

Juha Hinkula is a software development lecturer at Haaga-Helia University of Applied Sciences in Finland. He received an MSc degree in computer science from the University of Helsinki. He has over 15 years of industry experience in software development. Over the past few years, he has focused on modern full stack development. He is also a passionate mobile developer with Android-native technology, and nowadays also uses React Native.

About the reviewer

Krunal Patel has over 10 years of experience in enterprise application development using Java, Spring, Hibernate, and Liferay Portal. He has expertise in domains such as healthcare, insurance, and hospitality. He has executed many enterprise projects based on Liferay Portal that use Elasticsearch and LDAP integration. He was a co-author of *Java 9 Dependency Injection*, published by Packt Publishing, and also was a technical reviewer for books such as *Mastering Apache Solr 7.x* and *Spring 5.0 Blueprints*.

He received an ITIL® Foundation Certificate in IT Service Management in 2015, a Liferay 6.1 Developer Certification in 2013, was Brainbench Java 6 certified in 2013, and received a MongoDB for Java Developers certification in 2013.

I would like to thank my loving wife, Jigna, my son, Dirgh, and my friends. Thanks to the Packt team, especially Heta and Prajakta, for giving me this opportunity.

Packt is searching for authors like you

If you're interested in becoming an author for Packt, please visit authors.packtpub.com and apply today. We have worked with thousands of developers and tech professionals, just like you, to help them share their insight with the global tech community. You can make a general application, apply for a specific hot topic that we are recruiting an author for, or submit your own idea.

Table of Contents

Preface

In this book, we will create a modern web application using Spring Boot 2.0 and React. We will start from the backend and develop a RESTful web service using Spring Boot and MariaDB. We will also secure the backend and create unit tests for it. The frontend will be developed using the React JavaScript library. Different third-party React components will be used to make the frontend more user friendly. Finally, the application will be deployed to Heroku. The book also demonstrates how to Dockerize our backend.

Who this book is for

This book is written for the following audiences:

- Frontend developers who want to learn full stack development
- Backend developers who want to learn full stack development
- Full stack developers who have used some other technologies
- Java developers who are familiar with Spring, but haven't ever built a full-stack application

What this book covers

Chapter 1, *Setting Up the Environment and Tools – Backend*, explains how to install the software needed for backend development and how to create your first Spring Boot application.

Chapter 2, *Dependency Injection*, introduces dependency injection and explains how to use it with Spring Boot.

Chapter 3, *Using JPA to Create and Access a Database*, introduces **Java Persistence API (JPA)**and explains how to create and access databases with Spring Boot.

Chapter 4, *Creating a RESTful Web Service with Spring Boot*, shows how to create RESTful web services using Spring Data REST.

Chapter 5, *Securing and Testing Your Backend*, explains how to secure your backend using Spring Security and **JSON Web Token (JWT)**.

Chapter 6, *Setting Up the Environment and Tools – Frontend*, explains how to install the software needed for frontend development.

Chapter 7, *Getting Started with React*, introduces the basics of the React library.

Chapter 8, *Consuming the REST API with React*, shows how to use REST APIs with React using the fetch API.

Chapter 9, *Useful Third-Party Components for React*, demonstrates some handy components that we'll use in our frontend development.

Chapter 10, *Setting Up the Frontend for Our Spring Boot RESTful Web Service,* explains how to set up the React app and Spring Boot backend for frontend development.

Chapter 11, *Adding CRUD Functionalities*, shows how to implement CRUD functionalities with the React frontend.

Chapter 12, *Styling the Frontend with React Material-UI*, shows how to polish the user interface using the React Material-UI component library.

Chapter 13, *Testing Your Frontend*, explains the basics of React frontend testing.

Chapter 14, *Securing Your Application*, explains how to secure the frontend using JWT.

Chapter 15, *Deploying Your Application*, demonstrates how to deploy an application to Heroku and how to use Docker containers.

Chapter 16, *Best Practices*, explains the basic technologies that are needed to become a full stack developer, and covers some basic best practices for software development.

To get the most out of this book

The reader should possess the following:

- Basic knowledge of using a terminal, such as PowerShell
- Basic knowledge of Java and JavaScript programming
- Basic knowledge of SQL databases
- Basic knowledge of HTML and CSS

Download the example code files

You can download the example code files for this book from your account at
`www.packt.com`. If you purchased this book elsewhere, you can visit
`www.packt.com/support` and register to have the files emailed directly to you.

You can download the code files by following these steps:

1. Log in or register at `www.packt.com`.
2. Select the **SUPPORT** tab.
3. Click on **Code Downloads & Errata**.
4. Enter the name of the book in the **Search** box and follow the onscreen instructions.

Once the file is downloaded, please make sure that you unzip or extract the folder using the latest version of:

- WinRAR/7-Zip for Windows
- Zipeg/iZip/UnRarX for Mac
- 7-Zip/PeaZip for Linux

The code bundle for the book is also hosted on GitHub at `https://github.com/PacktPublishing/Hands-On-Full-Stack-Development-with-Spring-Boot-2-and-React-Second-Edition`. In case there's an update to the code, it will be updated on the existing GitHub repository.

We also have other code bundles from our rich catalog of books and videos available at `https://github.com/PacktPublishing/`. Check them out!

Download the color images

We also provide a PDF file that has color images of the screenshots/diagrams used in this book. You can download it here: `https://www.packtpub.com/sites/default/files/downloads/9781838822361_ColorImages.pdf`.

Conventions used

There are a number of text conventions used throughout this book.

CodeInText: Indicates code words in text, database table names, folder names, filenames, file extensions, pathnames, dummy URLs, user input, and Twitter handles. Here is an example: "You can change the port in the application.properties file."

A block of code is set as follows:

```
@SpringBootApplication
public class CardatabaseApplication {
  private static final Logger logger =
LoggerFactory.getLogger(CardatabaseApplication.class);
  public static void main(String[] args) {
    SpringApplication.run(CardatabaseApplication.class, args);
    logger.info("Hello Spring Boot");
  }
}
```

When we wish to draw your attention to a particular part of a code block, the relevant lines or items are set in bold:

```
import React from 'react';

const MyComponent = () => {
  // This is called when the button is pressed
  const buttonPressed = () => {
    alert('Button pressed');
  }
```

Any command-line input or output is written as follows:

```
npx create-react-app myapp
```

Bold: Indicates a new term, an important word, or words that you see onscreen. For example, words in menus or dialog boxes appear in the text like this. Here is an example: "Download the latest **Long-Term Support** (**LTS**) version for your operating system."

Warnings or important notes appear like this.

 Tips and tricks appear like this.

Get in touch

Feedback from our readers is always welcome.

General feedback: If you have questions about any aspect of this book, mention the book title in the subject of your message and email us at customercare@packtpub.com.

Errata: Although we have taken every care to ensure the accuracy of our content, mistakes do happen. If you have found a mistake in this book, we would be grateful if you would report this to us. Please visit www.packt.com/submit-errata, selecting your book, clicking on the Errata Submission Form link, and entering the details.

Piracy: If you come across any illegal copies of our works in any form on the Internet, we would be grateful if you would provide us with the location address or website name. Please contact us at copyright@packt.com with a link to the material.

If you are interested in becoming an author: If there is a topic that you have expertise in and you are interested in either writing or contributing to a book, please visit authors.packtpub.com.

Reviews

Please leave a review. Once you have read and used this book, why not leave a review on the site that you purchased it from? Potential readers can then see and use your unbiased opinion to make purchase decisions, we at Packt can understand what you think about our products, and our authors can see your feedback on their book. Thank you!

For more information about Packt, please visit packt.com.

1
Section 1: Backend Programming with Spring Boot

The reader will be familiar with the basics of Spring Boot. This section focuses on the knowledge and skills required to use databases and create RESTful web services.

This section covers the following chapters:

- Chapter 1, *Setting Up the Environment and Tools – Backend*
- Chapter 2, *Dependency Injection*
- Chapter 3, *Using JPA to Create and Access a Database*
- Chapter 4, *Creating a RESTful Web Service with Spring Boot*
- Chapter 5, *Securing and Testing Your Backend*

Setting Up the Environment and Tools - Backend

1

In this chapter, we will set up the environment and tools needed for backend programming with Spring Boot. Spring Boot is a modern Java-based backend framework that makes development faster than traditional Java-based frameworks. With Spring Boot, you can make a standalone web application that has an embedded application server.

In this chapter, we will look into the following topics:

- Building an environment for Spring Boot development
- The basics of the Eclipse IDE and Maven
- Creating and running Spring Boot projects
- Problem solving when running Spring Boot applications

Technical requirements

The Java SDK, version 8 or higher, is necessary to use the Eclipse IDE. In this book, we are using the Windows operating system, but all tools are available for Linux and macOS as well.

Download the code for this chapter from GitHub: `https://github.com/PacktPublishing/Hands-On-Full-Stack-Development-with-Spring-Boot-2-and-React-Second-Edition/tree/master/Chapter01`.

Setting up the environment and tools

There are a lot of different **integrated development environment (IDE)** tools that you can use to develop Spring Boot applications. In this book, we are using Eclipse, which is an open source IDE for multiple programming languages. We will create our first Spring Boot project by using the Spring Initializr project starter page. The project is then imported into Eclipse and executed. Reading the console log is a crucial skill when developing Spring Boot applications.

Installing Eclipse

Eclipse is an open source programming IDE developed by the Eclipse Foundation. An installation package can be downloaded from `https://www.eclipse.org/downloads`. Eclipse is available for Windows, Linux, and macOS. You should download the latest version of the Eclipse IDE for Java EE developers.

You can either download a ZIP package of Eclipse or an installer package that executes the installation wizard. If using the ZIP package, you just have to extract the package to your local disk and it will contain an executable `Eclipse.exe` file that you can run by double-clicking on the file.

The basics of Eclipse and Maven

Eclipse is an IDE for multiple programming languages, such as Java, C++, and Python. Eclipse contains different perspectives for your needs. A perspective is a set of views and editors in the Eclipse workbench. The following screenshot shows common perspectives for Java development:

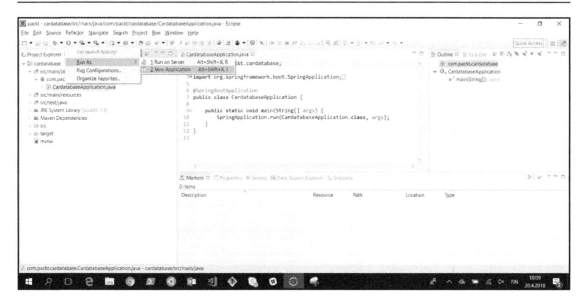

On the left-hand side, we have **Project Explorer**, where we can see our project structure and resources. **Project Explorer** is also used to open files by double-clicking on them. The files will be opened in the editor, which is located in the middle of the workbench. The **Console** view can be found in the lower section of the workbench. The **Console** view is really important because it shows application logging messages.

You can get **Spring Tool Suite (STS)** for Eclipse if you want, but we are not going to use it in this book, because the plain Eclipse installation is enough for our purposes. STS is a set of plugins that makes Spring application development simpler (`https://spring.io/tools`).

Apache Maven is a software project management tool. The basis of Maven is the **Project Object Model (POM)**. Maven makes the software development process simpler and it also unifies the development process. You can also use another project management tool, called **Gradle**, with Spring Boot, but in this book, we will focus on using Maven.

The POM is a `pom.xml` file that contains basic information about the project. There are also all the dependencies that Maven should download to be able to build the project.

Basic information about the project can be found at the beginning of the `pom.xml` file, which defines, for example, the version of the application, packaging format, and so on.

The minimum version of the `pom.xml` file should contain the project root, `modelVersion`, `groupId`, `artifactId`, and `version`.

Dependencies are defined in the `dependencies` section, as follows:

```xml
<?xml version="1.0" encoding="UTF-8"?>
<project xmlns="http://maven.apache.org/POM/4.0.0"
xmlns:xsi="http://www.w3.org/2001/XMLSchema-instance"
  xsi:schemaLocation="http://maven.apache.org/POM/4.0.0
http://maven.apache.org/xsd/maven-4.0.0.xsd">
  <modelVersion>4.0.0</modelVersion>

  <groupId>com.packt</groupId>
  <artifactId>cardatabase</artifactId>
  <version>0.0.1-SNAPSHOT</version>
  <packaging>jar</packaging>

  <name>cardatabase</name>
  <description>Demo project for Spring Boot</description>
  <parent>
    <groupId>org.springframework.boot</groupId>
    <artifactId>spring-boot-starter-parent</artifactId>
    <version>2.1.3.RELEASE</version>
    <relativePath/> <!-- lookup parent from repository -->
  </parent>

  <dependencies>
    <dependency>
      <groupId>org.springframework.boot</groupId>
      <artifactId>spring-boot-starter-web</artifactId>
    </dependency>

    <dependency>
      <groupId>org.springframework.boot</groupId>
      <artifactId>spring-boot-starter-test</artifactId>
      <scope>test</scope>
    </dependency>
  </dependencies>
</project>
```

Maven is normally used from the command line. Eclipse contains embedded Maven, and that handles all the Maven operations we need. Therefore, we are not focusing on Maven command-line usage here. The most important thing is to understand the structure of the `pom.xml` file and how to add new dependencies to it.

Creating a project with Spring Initializr

We will create our backend project with **Spring Initializr**, which is a web-based tool that's used to create **Spring Boot** projects. **Spring Initializr** can be found at `https://start.spring.io`:

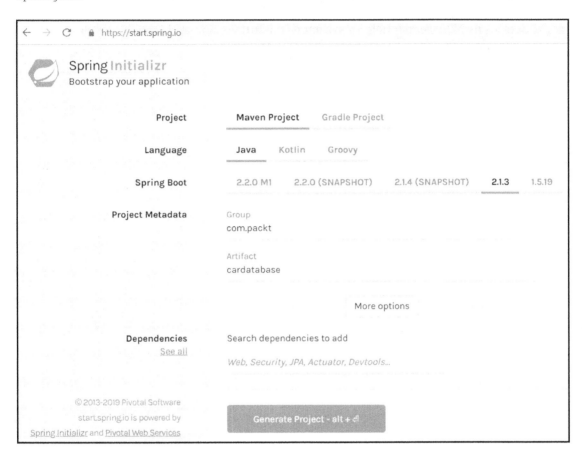

We will generate a **Maven Project** with **Java** and the latest **Spring Boot** version. In the **Group** field, we will define our group ID, which will also become a base package in our **Java** project. In the **Artifact** field, we will define the artifact ID, which will also be the name of our project in Eclipse.

In the **Dependencies** section, we will select the starters and dependencies that are needed in our project. **Spring Boot** provides starter packages that simplify your Maven configuration. **Spring Boot** starters are actually a set of dependencies that you can include in your project. You can either type the keyword of the dependency into the search field, or you can see all the available dependencies by clicking on the **See all** link. We will start our project by selecting two dependencies – **Web** and **DevTools**. You can type the dependencies into the search field or switch to the full version and see all the starter packages and dependencies available:

List of dependencies for **Spring Boot 2.1.3.RELEASE**

Core

☑ **DevTools**: Spring Boot Development Tools

☐ **Lombok**: Java annotation library which helps to reduce boilerplate code and code faster

☐ **Configuration Processor**: Generate metadata for your custom configuration keys

☐ **Session**: API and implementations for managing a user's session information

☐ **Cache**: Spring's Cache abstraction

☐ **Validation**: JSR-303 validation infrastructure (already included with web)

☐ **Retry**: Provide declarative retry support via spring-retry

☐ **Aspects**: Create your own Aspects using Spring AOP and AspectJ

Web

☑ **Web**: Servlet web application with Spring MVC and Tomcat

Update dependencies   Cancel

The **DevTools** dependency provides us with the Spring Boot development tools, which provide automatic restart functionality. It makes development much faster, because the application is automatically restarted when changes have been saved. The web starter pack is a base for full-stack development and provides embedded Tomcat.

Finally, you have to click on the **Generate Project** button, which generates the project starter ZIP package for us.

How to run the project

Perform the following steps to run a Maven project in the Eclipse IDE:

1. Extract the project ZIP package that we created in the previous topic and open Eclipse.
2. We are going to import our project into the Eclipse IDE. To start the import process, select the **File** | **Import** menu and the import wizard will be opened. The following screenshot shows the first page of the wizard:

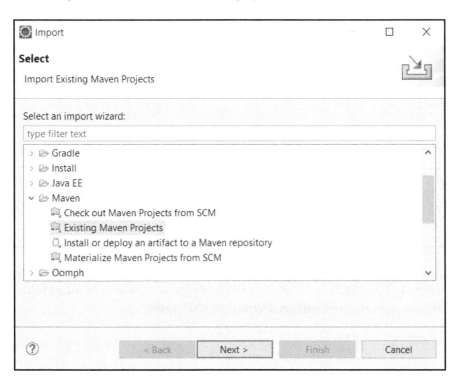

3. In the first phase, you should select **Existing Maven Projects** from the list under the `Maven` folder, and then go to the next phase by pressing the **Next** button. The following screenshot shows the second step of the import wizard:

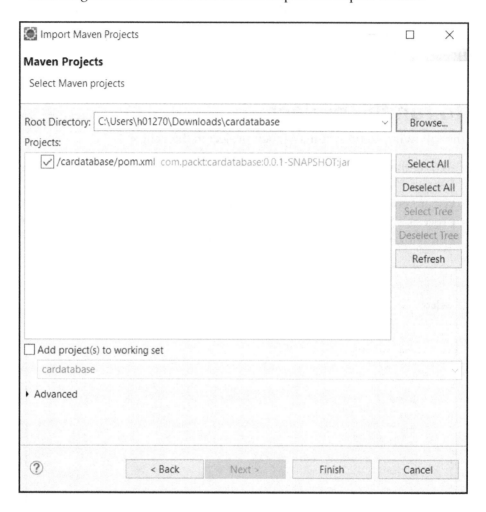

4. In this phase, select the extracted project folder by pressing the **Browse...** button. Then, Eclipse finds the `pom.xml` file from the root of your project folder and shows it inside the **Projects** section of the window.

5. Press the **Finish** button to finalize the import. If everything went correctly, you should see the `cardatabase` project in the Eclipse **Project Explorer**. It takes a while before the project is ready because all the dependencies will be loaded by Maven after importing. You can see the progress of the dependency download at the bottom-right corner of Eclipse. The following screenshot shows the Eclipse **Project Explorer** after a successful import:

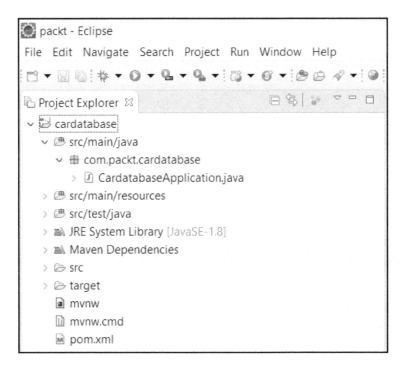

The **Project Explorer** also shows the package structure of our project, and now, at the beginning, there is only one package called `com.packt.cardatabase`. Under that package, is our main application class, called `CardatabaseApplication.java`.

6. Now, we don't have any functionality in our application, but we can run it and see whether everything has started successfully. To run the project, open the main class by double-clicking on it and then pressing the **Run** button in the Eclipse toolbar, or select the **Run** menu and press **Run as** | **Java Application**:

You can see the **Console** view open in Eclipse, and that contains important information about the execution of the project. This is the view where all log texts and error messages appear, so it is really important to check the content of the view when something goes wrong.

Now, if the project was executed correctly, you should see the `Started CardatabaseApplication in...` text at the end of the console. The following screenshot shows the content of the Eclipse console after our Spring Boot project has been started:

```
 /\\/ ___'_ _ _ _(_)_ __ __ _ \ \ \ \
( ( )\___ | '_ | '_| | '_ \/ _` | \ \ \ \
 \\/  ___)| |_)| | | | | || (_| |  ) ) ) )
  '  |____| .__|_| |_|_| |_\__, | / / / /
 =========|_|==============|___/=/_/_/_/
 :: Spring Boot ::        (v2.1.3.RELEASE)

2019-05-02 11:28:29.890  INFO 29412 --- [  restartedMain] c.p.cardatabase.CardatabaseApplication      : Starting CardatabaseApplication on HHMX4717 with
2019-05-02 11:28:29.894  INFO 29412 --- [  restartedMain] c.p.cardatabase.CardatabaseApplication      : No active profile set, falling back to default p
2019-05-02 11:28:29.956  INFO 29412 --- [  restartedMain] .e.DevToolsPropertyDefaultsPostProcessor    : Devtools property defaults active! Set 'spring.d
2019-05-02 11:28:29.956  INFO 29412 --- [  restartedMain] .e.DevToolsPropertyDefaultsPostProcessor    : For additional web related logging consider sett
2019-05-02 11:28:32.376  INFO 29412 --- [  restartedMain] o.s.b.w.embedded.tomcat.TomcatWebServer     : Tomcat initialized with port(s): 8080 (http)
2019-05-02 11:28:32.407  INFO 29412 --- [  restartedMain] o.apache.catalina.core.StandardService      : Starting service [Tomcat]
2019-05-02 11:28:32.407  INFO 29412 --- [  restartedMain] org.apache.catalina.core.StandardEngine     : Starting Servlet engine: [Apache Tomcat/9.0.16]
2019-05-02 11:28:32.422  INFO 29412 --- [  restartedMain] o.a.catalina.core.AprLifecycleListener      : The APR based Apache Tomcat Native library which
2019-05-02 11:28:32.526  INFO 29412 --- [  restartedMain] o.a.c.c.C.[Tomcat].[localhost].[/]          : Initializing Spring embedded WebApplicationConte
2019-05-02 11:28:32.526  INFO 29412 --- [  restartedMain] o.s.web.context.ContextLoader               : Root WebApplicationContext: initialization compl
2019-05-02 11:28:32.783  INFO 29412 --- [  restartedMain] o.s.s.concurrent.ThreadPoolTaskExecutor     : Initializing ExecutorService 'applicationTaskExe
2019-05-02 11:28:33.049  INFO 29412 --- [  restartedMain] o.s.b.d.a.OptionalLiveReloadServer          : LiveReload server is running on port 35729
2019-05-02 11:28:33.101  INFO 29412 --- [  restartedMain] o.s.b.w.embedded.tomcat.TomcatWebServer     : Tomcat started on port(s): 8080 (http) with cont
2019-05-02 11:28:33.106  INFO 29412 --- [  restartedMain] c.p.cardatabase.CardatabaseApplication      : Started CardatabaseApplication in 3.623 seconds
```

In the root of our project, there is the pom.xml file, which is the Maven configuration file for our project. If you look at the dependencies inside the file, you can see that there are now dependencies that we selected on the **Spring Initializr** page. There is also a test dependency included automatically without any selection. In the following chapters, we are going to add more functionality to our application, and then we will add more dependencies manually to the pom.xml file:

```
<dependencies>
  <dependency>
    <groupId>org.springframework.boot</groupId>
    <artifactId>spring-boot-starter-web</artifactId>
  </dependency>
  <dependency>
    <groupId>org.springframework.boot</groupId>
    <artifactId>spring-boot-devtools</artifactId>
    <scope>runtime</scope>
  </dependency>
  <dependency>
    <groupId>org.springframework.boot</groupId>
    <artifactId>spring-boot-starter-test</artifactId>
    <scope>test</scope>
  </dependency>
</dependencies>
```

Let's look at the Spring Boot main class more carefully. At the beginning of the class, there is the `@SpringBootApplication` annotation. It is actually a combination of multiple annotations, such as the following:

Annotation	Description
`@EnableAutoConfiguration`	This enables Spring Boot automatic configuration. Spring Boot will automatically configure your project based on dependencies. For example, if you have the `spring-boot-starter-web` dependency, Spring Boot assumes that you are developing a web application and configures your application accordingly.
`@ComponentScan`	This enables the Spring Boot component scan to find all the components of your application.
`@Configure`	This defines the class that can be used as a source of bean definitions.

The following code shows the Spring Boot application's `main` class:

```
import org.springframework.boot.SpringApplication;
import org.springframework.boot.autoconfigure.SpringBootApplication;

@SpringBootApplication
public class CardatabaseApplication {

  public static void main(String[] args) {
    SpringApplication.run(CardatabaseApplication.class, args);
  }
}
```

The execution of the application starts from the `main` method, as in standard Java applications.

 It is recommended that you locate the `main` application class in the root package above other classes. A common reason for an application to not work correctly is due to Spring Boot being unable to find some critical classes.

Spring Boot development tools

Spring Boot development tools make the application development process simpler. Projects will include the developer tools if the following dependency is added to the Maven `pom.xml` file:

```
<dependency>
    <groupId>org.springframework.boot</groupId>
    <artifactId>spring-boot-devtools</artifactId>
<scope>runtime</scope>
</dependency>
```

Development tools are disabled when you create a fully-packed production version of your application.

The application is automatically restarted when you make changes to your project's classpath files. You can test that by adding one comment line to your `main` class:

```
package com.packt.cardatabase;

import org.springframework.boot.SpringApplication;
import org.springframework.boot.autoconfigure.SpringBootApplication;

@SpringBootApplication
public class CardatabaseApplication {

  public static void main(String[] args) {
    // After adding this comment the application is restarted
    SpringApplication.run(CardatabaseApplication.class, args);
  }
}
```

After saving the file, you can see in the console that the application has restarted.

Logs and problem solving

Spring Boot starter packages provide a logback that we can use for logging without any configuration. The following sample code shows how you can use logging:

```
import org.slf4j.Logger;
import org.slf4j.LoggerFactory;
import org.springframework.boot.SpringApplication;
import org.springframework.boot.autoconfigure.SpringBootApplication;

@SpringBootApplication
```

```
public class CardatabaseApplication {
  private static final Logger logger =
LoggerFactory.getLogger(CardatabaseApplication.class);
  public static void main(String[] args) {
    SpringApplication.run(CardatabaseApplication.class, args);
    logger.info("Hello Spring Boot");
  }
}
```

Logging messages can be seen in the console after you run the project:

There are seven different levels of logging—TRACE, DEBUG, INFO, WARN, ERROR, FATAL, and OFF. You can configure the level of logging in your Spring Boot application.properties file. The file can be found in the resources folder inside your project:

If we set the logging level to `INFO`, we can see log messages from levels that are under `INFO` (`INFO`, `WARN`, `ERROR`, and `FATAL`). In the following example, we set the log level for the root, but you can also set it at the package level:

```
logging.level.root=INFO
```

Now, when you run the project, you can't see the `TRACE` and `DEBUG` messages anymore. That might be a good setting for a production version of your application:

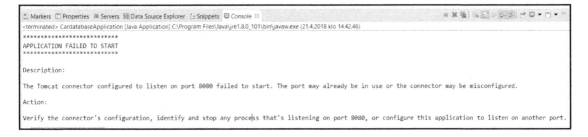

Spring Boot uses Apache Tomcat (`http://tomcat.apache.org/`) as an application server by default. As a default, Tomcat is running on port `8080`. You can change the port in the `application.properties` file. The following setting will start Tomcat on port `8081`:

```
server.port=8081
```

If the port is occupied, the application won't start, and you will see the following message in the console:

```
 Markers  Properties  Servers  Data Source Explorer  Snippets  Console 
<terminated> CardatabaseApplication [Java Application] C:\Program Files\Java\jre1.8.0_101\bin\javaw.exe (21.4.2018 klo 14.42.46)
****************************
APPLICATION FAILED TO START
****************************

Description:

The Tomcat connector configured to listen on port 8080 failed to start. The port may already be in use or the connector may be misconfigured.

Action:

Verify the connector's configuration, identify and stop any process that's listening on port 8080, or configure this application to listen on another port.
```

If this happens, you will have to stop the process that is listening on port `8080` or use another port in your Spring Boot application.

Installing MariaDB

In Chapter 3, *Using JPA to Create and Access a Database*, we are going to use MariaDB, so you will need to install it locally on your computer. MariaDB is a widely used open source relational database. MariaDB is available for Windows and Linux, and you can download the latest stable version from https://downloads.mariadb.org/. MariaDB is developed under a GNU GPLv2 license.

For Windows, there is the MSI installer, which we will use here. Download the installer and execute it. Install all features from the installation wizard:

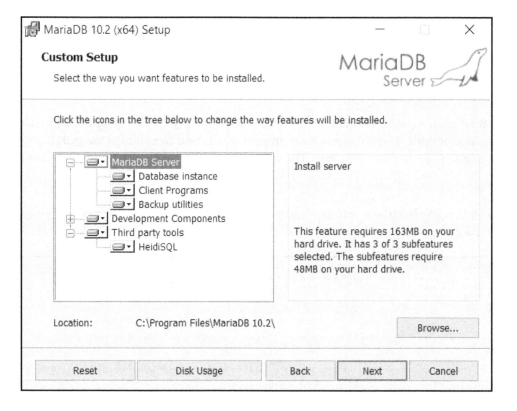

In the next step, you should give the password for the **root** user. This password is needed in the next chapter, when we'll connect our application to the database:

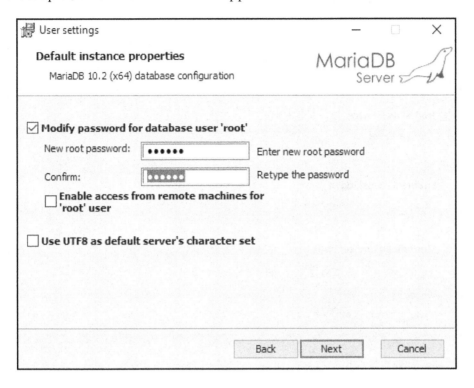

In the next phase, we can use the default settings:

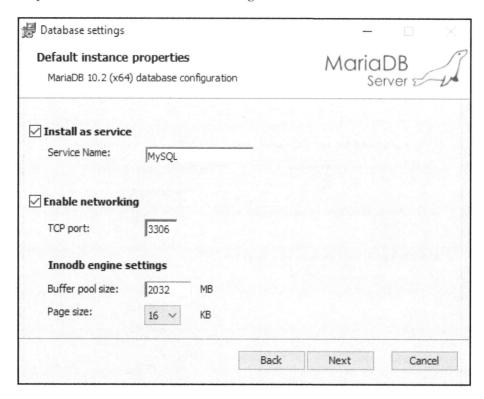

Now the installation will start, and MariaDB will be installed on your local computer. The installation wizard will install **HeidiSQL** for us. This is a graphically easy-to-use database client. We will use this to add a new database and make queries to our database. You can also use the Command Prompt included in the installation package:

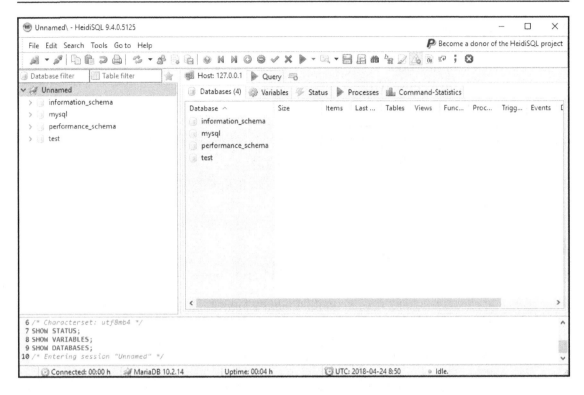

Now, we have everything that is needed to start the implementation of the backend.

Summary

In this chapter, we installed the tools that are needed for backend development with Spring Boot. For Java development, we used the Eclipse IDE, which is a widely used programming IDE. We created a new Spring Boot project by using the **Spring Initializr** page. After creating the project, it was imported to Eclipse and, finally, executed. We also covered how to solve common problems with Spring Boot and how to find important error and log messages. Finally, we installed a MariaDB database, which we are going to use in the following chapters.

In the next chapter, we will understand what dependency injection is and how it can be used with the Spring Boot framework.

Questions

1. What is Spring Boot?
2. What is the Eclipse IDE?
3. What is Maven?
4. How do we create a Spring Boot project?
5. How do we run a Spring Boot project?
6. How do we use logging with Spring Boot?
7. How do we find error and log messages in Eclipse?

Further reading

Packt has other great resources for learning about Spring Boot:

- *Learning Spring Boot 2.0 – Second Edition* by Greg L. Turnquist (`https://www.packtpub.com/application-development/learning-spring-boot-20-second-edition`)
- *Spring Boot – Getting Started* [Integrated Course] by Patrick Cornelissen (`https://www.packtpub.com/web-development/spring-boot-getting-started-integrated-course`)

2
Dependency Injection

In this chapter, we will learn what **Dependency Injection** (**DI**) means and how we can use it with the Spring Boot framework. The Spring Boot framework provides DI; therefore it is good to understand the basics of DI. DI reduces component dependencies and makes your code easier to test and maintain.

In this chapter, we will look into the following:

- The basics of DI
- How to use DI with Spring Boot

Technical requirements

Java SDK version 8 or higher is necessary to use Eclipse IDE. In this book, we are using the Windows operating system, but all the tools are available for Linux and macOS as well.

All of the code for this chapter can be found at the following GitHub link: `https://github.com/PacktPublishing/Hands-On-Full-Stack-Development-with-Spring-Boot-2-and-React-Second-Edition/tree/master/Chapter02`.

Introducing DI

DI is a software development technique where we can create objects that depend on other objects. DI helps the interaction between classes, but at the same time keeps the classes independent.

There are three types of classes in DI:

- A **Service** is a class that can be used (dependency).
- The **Client** is a class that uses dependency.
- The **Injector** passes the dependency (**Service**) to the dependent class (**Client**).

The three types of classes in DI are shown in the following diagram:

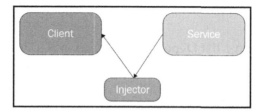

DI makes classes loosely coupled. This means that the creation of client dependencies is separated from the client's behavior, which makes unit testing easier.

Let's take a look at a simplified example of DI using Java code. In the following code, we don't have DI, because the client Car class is creating an object of the service class:

```java
public class Car {
    private Owner owner;
    public Car() {
        owner = new Owner();
    }
}
```

In the following code, the service object is not directly created in the client class. It is passed as a parameter in the class constructor:

```java
public class Car {
    private Owner owner;
    public Car(Owner owner) {
        this.owner = owner;
    }
}
```

The service class can also be some abstract class, then we can use any implementation of that in our client class and use mocks when testing.

There are different types of DI, for example, the following two types:

- **Constructor injection**: Dependencies are passed to a client class constructor. An example of the constructor injection was already shown in the preceding Car example code.
- **Setter injection**: Dependencies are provided through setters. The following example code shows an example of the setter injection:

```
public class Car {
    private Owner owner;
    public void setOwner(Owner owner) {
        this.owner = owner;
    }
}
```

DI in Spring Boot

Spring Boot scans your application classes and register classes with certain annotations (@Service, @Repository, @Controller) as Spring Beans. These beans can then be injected using an @Autowired annotation:

```
public class Car {
    @Autowired
    private Owner owner;
    ...
}
```

A fairly common situation is where we need database access for some operations, and, in Spring Boot, we are using repository classes for that. In this situation, we can inject repository class and start to use its methods:

```
public class Car {
    @Autowired
    private CarRepository carRepository;
    // Fetch all cars from db
    carRepositoty.findAll();
    ...
}
```

Java (`javax.annotation`) also provides a `@Resource` annotation that can be used to inject resources. You can define the name or type of the injected bean when using resource annotation. For example, the following code shows some use cases. Imagine that we have a resource that is defined as this code:

```
@Configuration
public class ConfigFileResource {

    @Bean(name="configFile")
    public File configFile() {
        File configFile = new File("configFile.xml");
        return configFile;
    }
}
```

We can then inject the bean by using a `@Resource` annotation:

```
// By bean name
@Resource(name="configFile")
private ConfigFile cFile

OR

// Without name
@Resource
private ConfigFile cFile
```

We have now gone through the basics of DI. We will put this into practice in the following chapters.

Summary

In this chapter, we learned what DI means. We also learned how to use DI in the Spring Boot framework that we are using in our backend.

In the next chapter, we will look at how we can use **Java Persistent API (JPA)** with Spring Boot and how to set up the MariaDB database. We will also learn about the creation of CRUD repositories and the one-to-many connection between database tables.

Questions

1. What is DI?
2. How do you use DI in Spring Boot?

Further reading

Packt has other great resources for learning about Spring Boot:

- *Learning Spring Boot 2.0 – Second Edition* by Greg L. Turnquist (`https://www.packtpub.com/application-development/learning-spring-boot-20-second-edition`)
- *Spring Boot – Getting Started* by Patrick Cornelissen (`https://www.packtpub.com/web-development/spring-boot-getting-started-integrated-course`)

3
Using JPA to Create and Access a Database

This chapter covers how to use **Java Persistent API (JPA)** with Spring Boot and how to define a database by using entity classes. In the first phase, we will be using the H2 in-memory database for development and demonstration purposes. H2 is an in-memory SQL database that is really good for fast development or demonstration purposes. In the second phase, we will move from H2 to use MariaDB. This chapter also describes the creation of CRUD repositories and a one-to-many connection between database tables.

In this chapter, we will cover the following topics:

- Basics of **Object-Relational Mapping (ORM)**, JPA, and Hibernate
- Creating the entity classes
- Creating CRUD repositories
- Relationships between tables
- Setting up the MariaDB database

Technical requirements

Java SDK version 8 or higher is necessary to use Spring Boot (http://www.oracle.com/technetwork/java/javase/downloads/index.html). A MariaDB installation is necessary for the creation of the database application which can be downloaded from: https://downloads.mariadb.org/.

The code for this chapter can be found at the following GitHub link: https://github.com/PacktPublishing/Hands-On-Full-Stack-Development-with-Spring-Boot-2.0-and-React-Second-Edition/tree/master/Chapter03

Basics of ORM, JPA, and Hibernate

ORM is a technique that allows you to fetch from and manipulate a database by using an object-oriented programming paradigm. ORM is really good for programmers, because it relies on object-oriented concepts rather than database structure. It also makes development much faster and reduces the amount of source code. ORM is mostly independent of databases, and developers don't have to worry about vendor-specific SQL statements.

JPA provides object-relational mapping for Java developers. The JPA entity is a Java class that presents the structure of a database table. The fields of an entity class present the columns of the database tables.

Hibernate is the most popular Java-based JPA implementation, and is used in Spring Boot as a default. Hibernate is a mature product, and is widely used in large-scale applications.

Creating the entity classes

An entity class is a simple Java class that is annotated with JPA's @Entity annotation. Entity classes use the standard JavaBean naming convention and have proper getter and setter methods. The class fields have private visibility.

JPA creates a database table called by the name of the class when the application is initialized. If you want to use some other name for the database table, you can use the @Table annotation.

To be able to use JPA and the H2 database, we have to add the following dependencies to the pom.xml file:

```
<dependency>
   <groupId>org.springframework.boot</groupId>
   <artifactId>spring-boot-starter-data-jpa</artifactId>
</dependency>
<dependency>
    <groupId>com.h2database</groupId>
    <artifactId>h2</artifactId>
    <scope>runtime</scope>
</dependency>
```

Let's look at the following steps to create entity classes:

1. To create an entity class in Spring Boot, we will first create our own package for entities. The package should be created under the root package.

2. Activate the root package in Eclipse **Project Explorer** and right-click to show a menu.

3. From the menu, select **New** | **Package**. The following screenshot shows the creation of a package for entity classes:

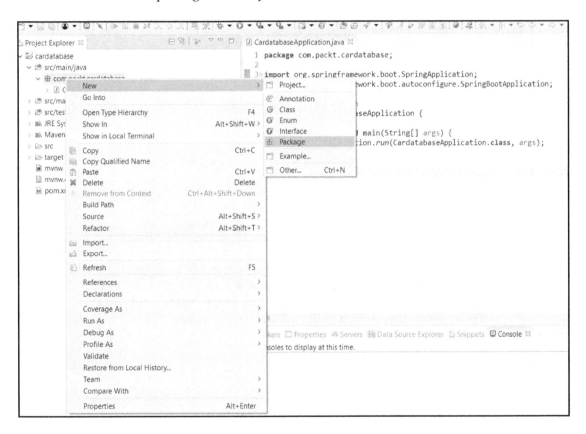

4. We will name our package `com.packt.cardatabase.domain`:

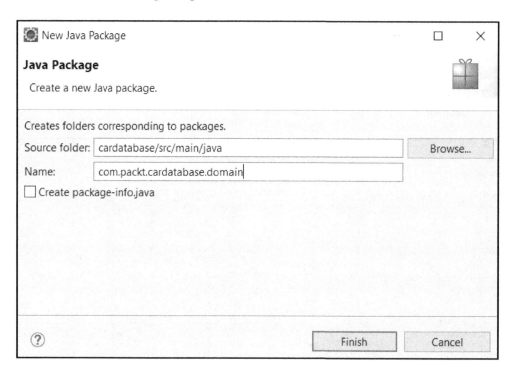

5. Next, we create our entity class. Activate a new entity package, right-click, and select **New** | **Class** from the menu. Because we are going to create a car database, the name of the entity class is `Car`. Type `Car` in the **Name** field and then press the **Finish** button, as shown in the following screenshot:

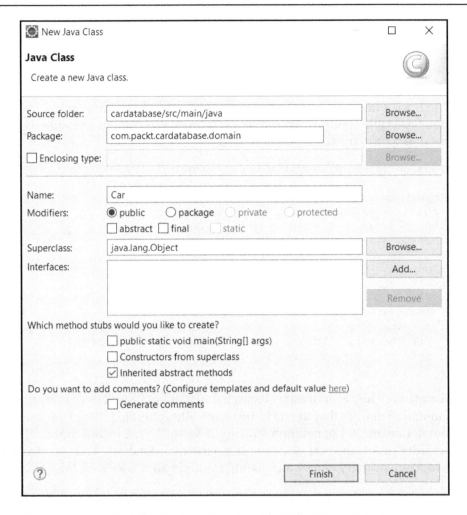

6. Open the `Car` class file in the editor by double-clicking it in the project explorer. First, we have to annotate the class with the `@Entity` annotation. The `Entity` annotation is imported from the `javax.persistence` package:

```
package com.packt.cardatabase.domain;

import javax.persistence.Entity;

@Entity
public class Car {

}
```

You can use the *Ctrl + Shift + O* shortcut in Eclipse IDE to import missing packages automatically.

7. Next, we add some fields to our class. The entity class fields are mapped to database table columns. The entity class must also contain a unique ID that is used as a primary key in the database:

```
package com.packt.cardatabase.domain;

import javax.persistence.Entity;
import javax.persistence.GeneratedValue;
import javax.persistence.GenerationType;
import javax.persistence.Id;

@Entity
public class Car {
  @Id
  @GeneratedValue(strategy=GenerationType.AUTO)
  private long id;
  private String brand, model, color, registerNumber;
  private int year, price;
}
```

The primary key is defined by using the @Id annotation. The @GeneratedValue annotation defines that the ID is automatically generated by the database. We can also define our key generation strategy. The AUTO type means that the JPA provider selects the best strategy for a particular database. You can also create a composite primary key by annotating multiple attributes with the @Id annotation.

The database columns are named according to class field naming by default. If you want to use some other naming convention, you can use the @Column annotation. With the @Column annotation, you can also define the column's length and whether the column is nullable. The following code shows an example of using the @Column annotation. With this definition, the column's name in the database is explanation, the length of the column is 512, and it is not nullable:

```
@Column(name="explanation", nullable=false, length=512)
private String description
```

8. Finally, we add getters, setters, and constructors with attributes to the entity class. We don't need an ID field in our constructor due to automatic ID generation. The source code of the `Car` entity class constructors is as follows:

 Eclipse provides the automatic addition of getters, setters, and constructors. Activate your cursor inside the class and right-click. From the menu, select **Source | Generate Getters and Setters...** or **Source | Generate Constructor using fields...**.

```
package com.packt.cardatabase.domain;

import javax.persistence.Entity;
import javax.persistence.GeneratedValue;
import javax.persistence.GenerationType;
import javax.persistence.Id;

@Entity
public class Car {
  @Id
  @GeneratedValue(strategy=GenerationType.AUTO)
  private long id;
  private String brand, model, color, registerNumber;
  private int year, price;
  public Car() {}
  public Car(String brand, String model, String color,
    String registerNumber, int year, int price) {
    super();
    this.brand = brand;
    this.model = model;
    this.color = color;
    this.registerNumber = registerNumber;
    this.year = year;
    this.price = price;
  }
```

The following is the source code of the `Car` entity class getters and setters:

```
  public String getBrand() {
    return brand;
  }
  public void setBrand(String brand) {
    this.brand = brand;
  }
  public String getModel() {
    return model;
  }
```

```
              public void setModel(String model) {
                this.model = model;
              }
              public String getColor() {
                return color;
              }
              public void setColor(String color) {
                this.color = color;
              }
              public String getRegisterNumber() {
                return registerNumber;
              }
              public void setRegisterNumber(String registerNumber) {
                this.registerNumber = registerNumber;
              }
              public int getYear() {
                return year;
              }
              public void setYear(int year) {
                this.year = year;
              }
              public int getPrice() {
                return price;
              }
              public void setPrice(int price) {
                this.price = price;
              }
          }
```

The table called `car` must be created in the database when we run the application. To ensure that, we will add one new property to the `application.properties` file. This allows us to log the SQL statements to the console:

```
      spring.jpa.show-sql=true
```

We can now see the table creation statements when running the application:

H2 provides a web-based console that can be used to explore a database and execute SQL statements. To enable the console, we have to add the following lines to the `application.properties` file. The first setting enables the H2 console and the second setting defines the endpoint that we can use to access the console:

```
spring.h2.console.enabled=true
spring.h2.console.path=/h2-console
```

You can access the H2 console by navigating to `localhost:8080/h2-console` with the web browser. Use `jdbc:h2:mem:testdb` as the **JDBC URL** and leave the **Password** field empty in the **Login** window. Press the **Connect** button to log in to the console, as shown in the following screenshot:

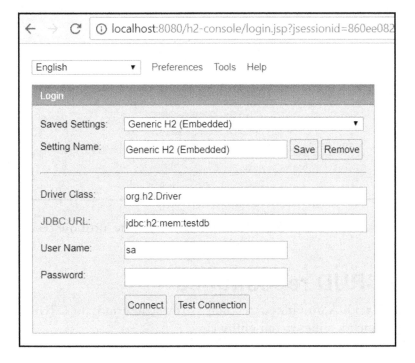

Now, you can see our CAR table in the database. You may notice that the register number has an underscore between the words:

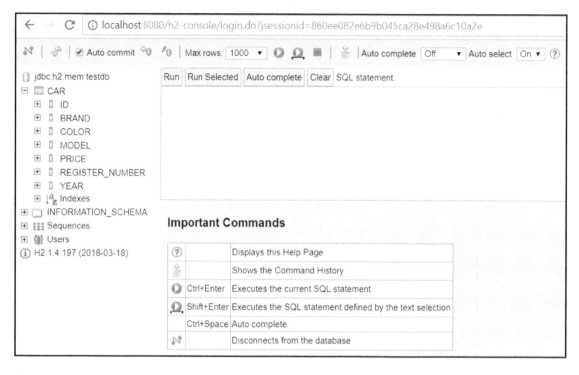

The reason for the underscore is the camel case naming of the attribute (registerNumber):

Creating CRUD repositories

The Spring Boot Data JPA provides a CrudRepository interface for CRUD operations. It provides CRUD functionalities to our entity class.

We will now create our repository in the domain package as follows:

1. Create a new class called CarRepository in the domain package and modify the file according to the following code snippet:

```
package com.packt.cardatabase.domain;

import org.springframework.data.repository.CrudRepository;
```

```
public interface CarRepository extends CrudRepository <Car, Long> {

}
```

Our `CarRepository` now extends the Spring Boot JPA `CrudRepository` interface. The `<Car, Long>` type arguments define that this is the repository for the `Car` entity class and the type of the ID field is `Long`.

`CrudRepository` provides multiple CRUD methods that we can now start to use. The following table lists the most commonly used methods:

Method	Description
`long count()`	Returns the number of entities
`Iterable<T> findAll()`	Returns all items of a given type
`Optional<T> findById(ID Id)`	Returns one item by id
`void delete(T entity)`	Deletes an entity
`void deleteAll()`	Deletes all entities of the repository
`<S extends T> save(S entity)`	Saves an entity

If the method returns only one item, the `Optional<T>` is returned instead of `T`. The `Optional` class gets introduced in Java 8 SE. `Optional` is a type of single value container that either has value or doesn't. By using `Optional`, we can prevent null pointer exceptions.

2. Now, we are ready to add some demonstration data to our H2 database. For that, we will use the Spring Boot `CommandLineRunner` interface. The `CommandLineRunner` interface allows us to execute additional code before the application has fully started. Therefore, it is a good point to add demo data to your database. `CommandLineRunner` is located inside the `main` class:

```
import org.springframework.boot.CommandLineRunner;
import org.springframework.boot.SpringApplication;
import org.springframework.boot.autoconfigure.SpringBootApplication;
import org.springframework.context.annotation.Bean;

@SpringBootApplication
public class CardatabaseApplication {

    public static void main(String[] args) {
        SpringApplication.run(CardatabaseApplication.class, args);
    }
    @Bean

    CommandLineRunner runner(){
```

```
        return args -> {
          // Place your code here
        };
      }
    }
```

3. Next, we have to inject our car repository into the main class to be able to save new `car` objects to the database. An `@Autowired` annotation is used to enable dependency injection. The dependency injection allows us to pass dependencies into an object. After we have injected the repository class, we can use the CRUD methods it provides. The following sample code shows how to insert a few cars to the database:

```java
import org.springframework.beans.factory.annotation.Autowired;
import org.springframework.boot.CommandLineRunner;
import org.springframework.boot.SpringApplication;
import org.springframework.boot.autoconfigure.SpringBootApplication;
import org.springframework.context.annotation.Bean;

import com.packt.cardatabase.domain.Car;
import com.packt.cardatabase.domain.CarRepository;

@SpringBootApplication
public class CardatabaseApplication {
  @Autowired
  private CarRepository repository;
  public static void main(String[] args) {
    SpringApplication.run(CardatabaseApplication.class, args);
  }
  @Bean

  CommandLineRunner runner(){
    return args -> {
      // Save demo data to database
      repository.save(new Car("Ford", "Mustang", "Red",
        "ADF-1121", 2017, 59000));
      repository.save(new Car("Nissan", "Leaf", "White",
        "SSJ-3002", 2014, 29000));
      repository.save(new Car("Toyota", "Prius", "Silver",
        "KKO-0212", 2018, 39000));
    };
  }
}
```

The `Insert` statements can be seen in the Eclipse console after the application has been executed:

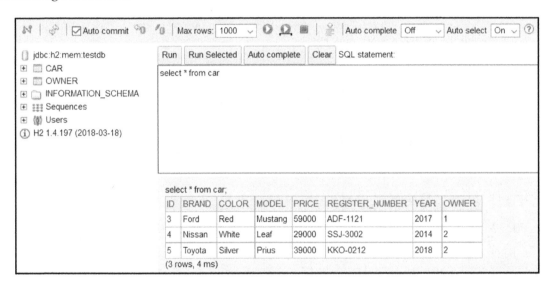

You can also use the H2 console to fetch cars from the database, as seen in the following screenshot:

You can define your own queries in the Spring Data repositories. The query must start with a prefix; for example, `findBy`. After the prefix, you define the entity class fields that are used in the query. The following is a sample code of three simple queries:

```
import java.util.List;

import org.springframework.data.repository.CrudRepository;

public interface CarRepository extends CrudRepository <Car, Long> {
  // Fetch cars by brand
  List<Car> findByBrand(String brand);
```

```
    // Fetch cars by color
    List<Car> findByColor(String color);

    // Fetch cars by year
    List<Car> findByYear(int year);

}
```

There can be multiple fields after the By keyword, concatenated with the And or Or keywords:

```
package com.packt.cardatabase.domain;

import java.util.List;

import org.springframework.data.repository.CrudRepository;

public interface CarRepository extends CrudRepository <Car, Long> {
    // Fetch cars by brand and model
    List<Car> findByBrandAndModel(String brand, String model);

    // Fetch cars by brand or color
    List<Car> findByBrandOrColor(String brand, String color);
}
```

Queries can be sorted by using the OrderBy keyword in the query method:

```
package com.packt.cardatabase.domain;

import java.util.List;

import org.springframework.data.repository.CrudRepository;

public interface CarRepository extends CrudRepository <Car, Long> {
    // Fetch cars by brand and sort by year
    List<Car> findByBrandOrderByYearAsc(String brand);
}
```

You can also create queries by using SQL statements via the @Query annotation. The following example shows the usage of a SQL query in CrudRepository:

```
package com.packt.cardatabase.domain;

import java.util.List;

import org.springframework.data.repository.CrudRepository;

public interface CarRepository extends CrudRepository <Car, Long> {
```

```
// Fetch cars by brand using SQL
@Query("select c from Car c where c.brand = ?1")
List<Car> findByBrand(String brand);
}
```

You can also use more advanced expressions with the `@Query` annotation; for example, `like`. The following example shows the usage of the `like` query in `CrudRepository`:

```
package com.packt.cardatabase.domain;

import java.util.List;

import org.springframework.data.repository.CrudRepository;

public interface CarRepository extends CrudRepository <Car, Long> {
    // Fetch cars by brand using SQL
    @Query("select c from Car c where c.brand like %?1")
    List<Car> findByBrandEndsWith(String brand);
}
```

Spring Data JPA also provides `PagingAndSortingRepository`, which extends `CrudRepository`. This offers methods to fetch entities using pagination and sorting. This is a good option if you are dealing with larger amounts of data. `PagingAndSortingRepository` can be created in a similar way to how we created `CrudRepository`:

```
package com.packt.cardatabase.domain;

import org.springframework.data.repository.PagingAndSortingRepository;

public interface CarRepository extends PagingAndSortingRepository<Car,
Long> {

}
```

In this case, you now have the two new additional methods that the repository provides:

Method	Description
`Iterable<T> findAll(Sort sort)`	Returns all entities sorted by the given options
`Page<T> findAll(Pageable pageable)`	Returns all entities according to given paging options

Now, we have completed our first database table and we are ready to add relationships between the database tables.

Relationships between tables

Next, we create a new table called `owner` that has a one-to-many relationship with the `car` table. The owner can own multiple cars, but a car can have only one owner. The following **Unified Modeling Language (UML)** diagram shows the relationship between the tables:

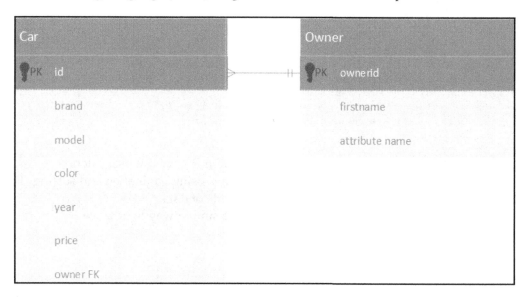

The following are the steps to create a new table:

1. First, we create the `Owner` entity and repository in the `domain` package. The `Owner` entity and repository are created in a similar way to the `Car` class. The following is the source code of the `Owner` entity class and `OwnerRepository`:

   ```
   // Owner.java

   package com.packt.cardatabase.domain;

   import javax.persistence.Entity;
   import javax.persistence.GeneratedValue;
   import javax.persistence.GenerationType;
   import javax.persistence.Id;

   @Entity
   ```

```java
public class Owner {
  @Id
  @GeneratedValue(strategy=GenerationType.AUTO)
  private long ownerid;
  private String firstname, lastname;
  public Owner() {}
  public Owner(String firstname, String lastname) {
    super();
    this.firstname = firstname;
    this.lastname = lastname;
  }

  public long getOwnerid() {
    return ownerid;
  }
  public void setOwnerid(long ownerid) {
    this.ownerid = ownerid;
  }
  public String getFirstname() {
    return firstname;
  }
  public void setFirstname(String firstname) {
    this.firstname = firstname;
  }
  public String getLastname() {
    return lastname;
  }
  public void setLastname(String lastname) {
    this.lastname = lastname;
  }
}
```

The following is the source code of the OwnerRepository:

```java
// OwnerRepository.java

package com.packt.cardatabase.domain;

import org.springframework.data.repository.CrudRepository;
public interface OwnerRepository extends CrudRepository<Owner, Long>
{

}
```

2. In this phase, it is good to check that everything is done correctly. Run the project and check that both database tables are created and that there are no errors in the console. The following screenshot shows the console messages when tables are created:

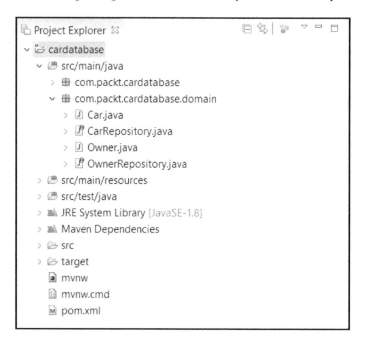

Now, our domain package contains two entity classes and repositories:

3. The one-to-many relationship can be added by using the @ManyToOne and @OneToMany annotations. In the car entity class, which contains a foreign key, you will define the relationship with the @ManyToOne annotation. You should also add the getter and setter for the owner field. It is recommended that you use FetchType.LAZY for all associations. For the toMany relationships, that is the default value, but for the toOne relationships, you should define it. FetchType defines the strategy for fetching data from the database. The value can be either EAGER or LAZY. In our case, the lazy strategy means that when the owner is fetched from the database, all the cars associated with the owner will be fetched when needed. Eager means that the cars will be fetched immediately with the owner. The following source code shows how to define a one-to-many relationship in the Car class:

```
// Car.java

@ManyToOne(fetch = FetchType.LAZY)
@JoinColumn(name = "owner")
private Owner owner;

//Getter and setter
public Owner getOwner() {
  return owner;
}

public void setOwner(Owner owner) {
  this.owner = owner;
}
```

In the owner entity site, the relationship is defined with the @OneToMany annotation. The type of the field is List<Car>, because the owner may have multiple cars. You can now add the getter and setter for that as follows:

```
// Owner.java

@OneToMany(cascade = CascadeType.ALL, mappedBy="owner")
private List<Car> cars;

//Getter and setter
public List<Car> getCars() {
  return cars;
}
public void setCars(List<Car> cars) {
  this.cars = cars;
}
```

The @OneToMany annotation has two attributes that we are using. The cascade attribute defines how cascading affects the entities. The ALL attribute setting means that, if the owner is deleted, the cars linked to that owner are deleted as well. The mappedBy="owner" attribute setting tells us that the Car class has the owner field, which is the foreign key for this relationship.

When you run the project, you can see from the console that the relationship is now created:

4. Now, we can add some owners to the database with CommandLineRunner. Let's also modify the Car entity classes constructor and add an owner object there:

```
// Car.java constructor

public Car(String brand, String model, String color,
String registerNumber, int year, int price, Owner owner) {
   super();
   this.brand = brand;
   this.model = model;
   this.color = color;
   this.registerNumber = registerNumber;
   this.year = year;
   this.price = price;
   this.owner = owner;
}
```

5. We first create two `owner` objects and save these to the database. In order to save the owners, we also have to inject the `OwnerRepository` into the `main` class. Then, we will connect the owners to the cars by using the `Car` constructor. The following is the source code of the application's main `CardatabaseApplication` class:

```
@SpringBootApplication
public class CardatabaseApplication {
  // Inject repositories
  @Autowired
  private CarRepository repository;

  @Autowired
  private OwnerRepository orepository;
  public static void main(String[] args) {
    SpringApplication.run(CardatabaseApplication.class, args);
  }
  @Bean

  CommandLineRunner runner() {
    return args -> {
      // Add owner objects and save these to db
      Owner owner1 = new Owner("John" , "Johnson");
      Owner owner2 = new Owner("Mary" , "Robinson");
      orepository.save(owner1);
      orepository.save(owner2);
      // Add car object with link to owners and save these to db.
      Car car = new Car("Ford", "Mustang", "Red",
          "ADF-1121", 2017, 59000, owner1);
      repository.save(car);
      car = new Car("Nissan", "Leaf", "White",
          "SSJ-3002", 2014, 29000, owner2);
      repository.save(car);
      car = new Car("Toyota", "Prius", "Silver",
          "KKO-0212", 2018, 39000, owner2);
      repository.save(car);
    };
  }
}
```

If you now run the application and fetch cars from the database, you can see that the owners are now linked to the cars:

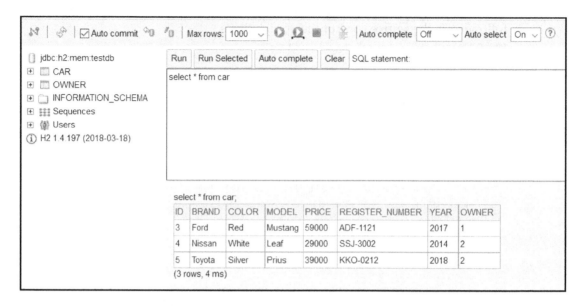

If you want to create a many-to-many relationship instead, which means, in practice, that an owner can have multiple cars and a car can have multiple owners, you should use the @ManyToMany annotation. In our example application, we will use a one-to-many relationship, and learn how to change the relationship to many-to-many. In a many-to-many relationship, it is recommended what you use Set instead of List with Hibernate:

1. In the Car entity class many-to-many relationship, define the getters and setters in the following way:

```
@ManyToMany(mappedBy = "cars")
private Set<Owner> owners;

public Set<Owner> getOwners() {
  return owners;
}

public void setOwners(Set<Owner> owners) {
  this.owners = owners;
}
```

In the `owner` entity, the definition is as follows:

```
@ManyToMany(cascade = CascadeType.MERGE)
@JoinTable(name = "car_owner", joinColumns = { @JoinColumn(name =
  "ownerid") }, inverseJoinColumns = { @JoinColumn(name = "id") })
private Set<Car> cars = new HashSet<Car>(0);

public Set<Car> getCars() {
  return cars;
}

public void setCars(Set<Car> cars) {
  this.cars = cars;
}
```

2. Now, if you run the application, there will be a new join table that is created between the `car` and `owner` tables. The join table is defined by using the `@JoinTable` annotation. With this annotation, we can set the name of the join table and join columns. The following is a screenshot of the database structure when using a many-to-many relationship:

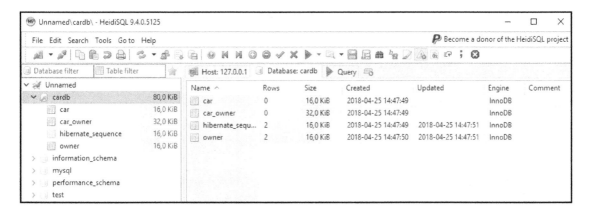

We have now used an in-memory H2 database, and we are now going to use a proper database instead of H2.

Setting up the MariaDB database

Now, we will switch our database from H2 to MariaDB. The database tables are still created automatically by JPA. But, before we run our application, we have to create a database for it. The database can be created by using HeidiSQL. Open HeidiSQL, and follow these steps:

1. Right-click your mouse inside the database list.
2. Then, select **Create new** | **Database**:

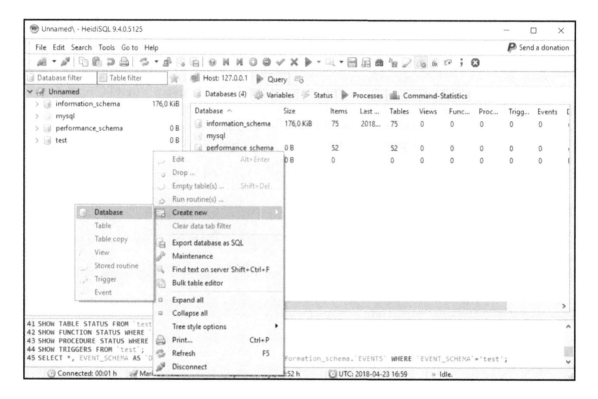

3. Let's name our database `cardb`. After you click **OK**, you should see the new `cardb` database in the database list:

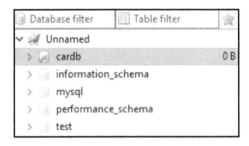

4. In the application, we add a MariaDB dependency to the `pom.xml` file and remove the H2 `dependency` injection that we don't need anymore:

```
<dependency>
  <groupId>org.mariadb.jdbc</groupId>
  <artifactId>mariadb-java-client</artifactId>
</dependency>
```

5. In the `application.properties` file, you will now define the database connection. First, you will define the database's `url`, `username`, `password`, and database driver class. The `spring.jpa.generate-ddl` setting defines whether JPA should initialize the database (`true`/`false`).
The `spring.jpa.hibernate.ddl-auto` setting defines the behavior of the database initialization. The possible values are `none`, `validate`, `update`, `create`, and `create-drop`. `create-drop` means that the database is created when an application starts and it is dropped when the application is stopped. `create-drop` is also the default value if you don't define any. The `create` value only creates the database when the application is started. The `update` value creates the database and updates the schema if it is changed:

```
spring.datasource.url=jdbc:mariadb://localhost:3306/cardb
spring.datasource.username=root
spring.datasource.password=YOUR_PASSWORD
spring.datasource.driver-class-name=org.mariadb.jdbc.Driver

spring.jpa.generate-ddl=true
spring.jpa.hibernate.ddl-auto=create-drop
```

6. After running the application, you should see the tables in MariaDB. The following screenshot shows the HeidiSQL user interface after the database has been created:

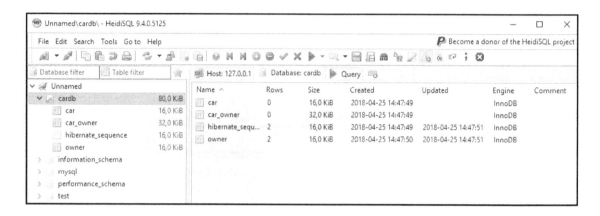

Now, your application is now ready to be used with MariaDB.

Summary

In this chapter, we used JPA to create our Spring Boot application database. First, we created entity classes, which are mapped to database tables. Then, we created `CrudRepository` for our entity class, which provides CRUD operations for the entity. After that, we managed to add some demo data to our database by using `CommandLineRunner`. We also created one-to-many relations between two entities. At the beginning of the chapter, we used the H2 in-memory database, while, at the end, we switched the database to MariaDB.

In the next chapter, we will create a RESTful web service for our backend. We will also look at testing the RESTful web service with the `curl` command-line tool, and also by using Postman GUI.

Questions

1. What are ORM, JPA, and Hibernate?
2. How can you create an entity class?
3. How can you create `CrudRepository`?
4. How does `CrudRepository` provide for your application?
5. How can you create a one-to-many relationship between tables?
6. How can you add demo data to a database with Spring Boot?
7. How can you access the H2 console?
8. How can you connect your Spring Boot application to MariaDB?

Further reading

Packt has other great resources for Spring Boot:

- *Learning Spring Boot 2.0 – Second Edition* by Greg L. Turnquist (`https://www.packtpub.com/application-development/learning-spring-boot-20-second-edition`)
- *Spring Boot – Getting Started* by Patrick Cornelissen (`https://www.packtpub.com/web-development/spring-boot-getting-started-integrated-course`)

4
Creating a RESTful Web Service with Spring Boot

In this chapter, we will first create a RESTful web service using the controller class. After that, we will demonstrate how to use Spring Data REST to create a RESTful web service that also covers all CRUD functionalities automatically. After you have created a RESTful API for your application, you can implement the frontend using a JavaScript library such as React. We are using the database application that we created in the previous chapter as a starting point.

Web services are applications that communicate over the internet using the HTTP protocol. There are many different types of web service architectures, but the principal idea across all designs is the same. In this book, we are creating a RESTful web service from what is nowadays a really popular design.

In this chapter, we will cover the following topics:

- Basics of a RESTful web service
- Creating a RESTful web service with Spring Boot
- Testing a RESTful web service

Technical requirements

The Spring Boot application created in previous chapters is required. Postman, cURL, or another suitable tool for transferring data using various HTTP methods is also necessary.

The following GitHub link will also be required: `https://github.com/PacktPublishing/Hands-On-Full-Stack-Development-with-Spring-Boot-2-and-React-Second-Edition/tree/master/Chapter04`.

Basics of REST

Representational State Transfer (REST) is an architectural style for creating web services. REST is not standard, but it defines a set of constraints defined by Roy Fielding. The six constraints are as follows:

- **Stateless**: The server doesn't hold any information about the client state.
- **Client server**: The client and server act independently. The server does not send any information without a request from the client.
- **Cacheable**: Many clients often request the same resources; therefore, it is useful to cache responses in order to improve performance.
- **Uniform interface**: Requests from different clients look the same. Clients may include, for example, a browser, a Java application, and a mobile application.
- **Layered system**: REST allows us to use a layered system architecture.
- **Code on demand**: This is an optional constraint.

The uniform interface is an important constraint and it stipulates that every REST architecture should have the following elements:

- **Identification of resources**: There are resources with their unique identifiers, for example, URIs in web-based REST services. REST resources should expose easily understood directory structure URIs. Therefore, a good resource naming strategy is very important.
- **Resource manipulation through representation**: When making a request to a resource, the server responds with a representation of the resource. Typically, the format of the representation is JSON or XML.
- **Self descriptive messages**: Messages should have sufficient information that the server knows how to process them.
- **Hypermedia and the Engine of Application State (HATEOAS)**: Responses can contain links to other areas of service.

The RESTful web service that we are going to develop in the following topics follows the REST architectural principles.

Creating a RESTful web service

In Spring Boot, all the HTTP requests are handled by controller classes. To be able to create a RESTful web service, first, we have to create a controller class. We will create our own Java package for our controller:

1. Activate the root package in the Eclipse **Project Explorer** and right-click. Select **New** | **Package** from the menu. We will name our new package com.packt.cardatabase.web:

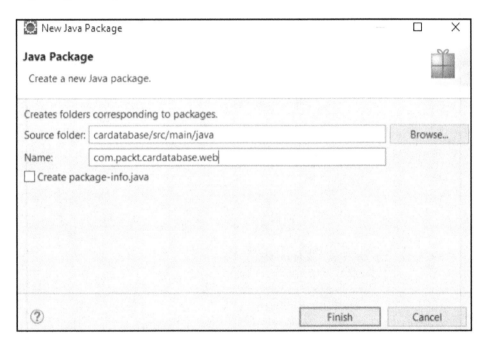

2. Next, we will create a new controller class in a new web package. Activate the `com.packt.cardatabase.web` package in the Eclipse project explorer and right-click. Select **New** | **Class** from the menu. We will name our class `CarController`:

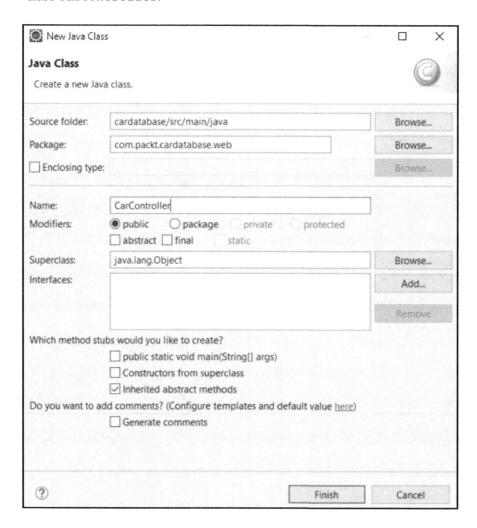

3. Now, your project structure should look like the following screenshot:

If you create classes in a wrong package accidentally, you can drag and drop the files between packages in the Eclipse **Project Explorer**. Sometimes, the Eclipse **Project Explorer** view might not be rendered correctly when you make some changes. Refreshing the project explorer helps (activate **Project Explorer** and press *F5*).

4. Open your controller class in the editor window and add the @RestController annotation before the class definition. Refer to the following source code. The @RestController annotation identifies that this class will be the controller for the RESTful web service:

```
package com.packt.cardatabase.web;

import org.springframework.web.bind.annotation.RestController;

@RestController
public class CarController {
}
```

5. Next, we add a new method inside our controller class. The method is annotated with the `@RequestMapping` annotation, which defines the endpoint that the method is mapped to. In the following code snippet, you can see the sample source code. In this example, when a user navigates to the `/cars` endpoint, the `getCars()` method is executed:

```
package com.packt.cardatabase.web;

import org.springframework.web.bind.annotation.RestController;

@RestController
public class CarController {
  @RequestMapping("/cars")
  public Iterable<Car> getCars() {
  }
}
```

The `getCars()` method returns all the car objects, which are then marshaled to JSON objects by the Jackson library.

By default, `@RequestMapping` handles all the HTTP method (`GET`, `PUT`, `POST`, and more) requests. You can define which method is accepted using the following `@RequestMapping("/cars", method=GET)` parameter. Now, this method handles only `GET` requests from the `/cars` endpoint.

6. To be able to return cars from the database, we have to inject our `CarRepository` into the controller. Then, we can use the `findAll()` method that the repository provides to fetch all cars. The following source code shows the controller code:

```
package com.packt.cardatabase.web;

import org.springframework.beans.factory.annotation.Autowired;
import org.springframework.web.bind.annotation.RequestMapping;
import org.springframework.web.bind.annotation.RestController;

import com.packt.cardatabase.domain.Car;
import com.packt.cardatabase.domain.CarRepository;

@RestController
public class CarController {
  @Autowired
  private CarRepository repository;
  @RequestMapping("/cars")
  public Iterable<Car> getCars() {
    return repository.findAll();
```

```
    }
  }
```

7. Now, we are ready to run our application and navigate to `localhost:8080/cars`. We can see that there is something wrong, and the application seems to be in an infinite loop. This happens on account of our one-to-many relationship between the `car` and `owner` tables. So, what happens in practice? First, the car is serialized, and it contains an owner who is then serialized, and that, in turn, contains cars that are then serialized and so on. To avoid this, we have to add the `@JsonIgnore` annotation to the `cars` field in the `Owner` class:

```java
// Owner.java
// ...
import com.fasterxml.jackson.annotation.JsonIgnore;
import com.fasterxml.jackson.annotation.JsonIgnoreProperties;

@Entity
@JsonIgnoreProperties({"hibernateLazyInitializer", "handler"})
public class Owner {
@Id
@GeneratedValue(strategy=GenerationType.AUTO)
private long ownerid;
private String firstname, lastname;

@OneToMany(cascade = CascadeType.ALL, mappedBy="owner")
@JsonIgnore
private List<Car> cars;
// continues...
```

8. Now, when you run the application and navigate to `localhost:8080/cars`, everything should go as expected and you will get all the cars from the database in JSON format, as shown in the following screenshot:

```
[ ▼ 3 items, 502 bytes
  { ▼ 7 properties, 164 bytes
    "brand": "Ford",
    "model": "Mustang",
    "color": "Red",
    "registerNumber": "ADF-1121",
    "year": 2017,
    "price": 59000,
    "owner": { ▼ 3 properties, 53 bytes
      "ownerid": 1,
      "firstname": "John",
      "lastname": "Johnson"
    }
  },
  { ▼ 7 properties, 166 bytes
    "brand": "Nissan",
    "model": "Leaf",
    "color": "White",
    "registerNumber": "SSJ-3002",
    "year": 2014,
    "price": 29000,
    "owner": { ▼ 3 properties, 54 bytes
      "ownerid": 2,
      "firstname": "Mary",
      "lastname": "Robinson"
    }
  },
  { ▼ 7 properties, 168 bytes
    "brand": "Toyota",
    "model": "Prius",
    "color": "Silver",
    "registerNumber": "KKO-0212",
    "year": 2018,
    "price": 39000,
    "owner": { ▼ 3 properties, 54 bytes
      "ownerid": 2,
      "firstname": "Mary",
      "lastname": "Robinson"
    }
```

We have done our first RESTful web service, which returns all the cars. Spring Boot provides a much more powerful way of creating RESTful web services and this is investigated in the next topic.

Using Spring Data REST

Spring Data REST is part of the Spring Data project. It offers an easy and fast way to implement RESTful web services with Spring. To start using Spring Data REST, you have to add the following dependency to the pom.xml file:

```
<dependency>
    <groupId>org.springframework.boot</groupId>
    <artifactId>spring-boot-starter-data-rest</artifactId>
</dependency>
```

By default, Spring Data REST finds all public repositories from the application and creates RESTful web services for your entities automatically.

You can define the endpoint of service in your application.properties file as follows:

```
spring.data.rest.basePath=/api
```

Now, you can access the RESTful web service from the localhost:8080/api endpoint. By calling the root endpoint of the service, it returns the resources that are available. Spring Data REST returns JSON data in the **Hypertext Application Language (HAL)** format. The HAL format provides a set of conventions for expressing hyperlinks in JSON and it makes your RESTful web service easier to use for frontend developers:

We can see that there are links to the car and owner entity services. The Spring Data REST service path name is derived from the entity name. The name will then be pluralized and uncapitalized. For example, the entity Car service path name will be named cars. The profile link is generated by Spring Data REST and contains application-specific metadata.

Now, we start to examine different services more carefully. There are multiple tools available for testing and consuming RESTful web services. In this book, we are using Postman, but you can use tools that you are familiar with, such as cURL. Postman can be acquired as a desktop application or as a browser plugin. cURL is also available for Windows 10 by using Windows Ubuntu Bash.

If you make a request to the `cars` endpoint, `http://localhost:8080/api/cars`, using the `GET` method, you will get a list of all the `cars`, as shown in the following screenshot:

In the JSON response, you can see that there is an array of `cars` and each car contains car-specific data. All the cars also have the "`_links`" attribute, which is a collection of links, and with these you can access the car itself or get the owner of the car. To access one specific car, the path will be `http://localhost:8080/api/cars/{id}`.

The request to `http://localhost:8080/api/cars/3/owner` returns the owner of the car. The response now contains owner data, a link to the owner, and links to other `cars` that the user owns:

```
GET  ∨      http://localhost:8080/api/cars/3/owner

Body    Cookies (1)    Headers (4)    Test Results

Pretty    Raw    Preview    JSON ∨    ⇥

 1 ▾ {
 2        "firstname": "John",
 3        "lastname": "Johnson",
 4 ▾      "_links": {
 5 ▾          "self": {
 6                  "href": "http://localhost:8080/api/owners/1"
 7              },
 8 ▾          "owner": {
 9                  "href": "http://localhost:8080/api/owners/1"
10              },
11 ▾          "cars": {
12                  "href": "http://localhost:8080/api/owners/1/cars"
13              }
14          }
15   }
```

Spring Data REST service provides all CRUD operations. The following table shows which HTTP methods you can use for different CRUD operations:

HTTP Method	CRUD
GET	Read
POST	Create
PUT/PATCH	Update
DELETE	Delete

Next, we will look at how to delete a car from the database by using our RESTful web service. In a delete operation, you have to use the DELETE method and the link to the car that will be deleted (`http://localhost:8080/api/cars/{id}`). The following screenshot shows how you can delete one car with the ID 4 by using cURL. After the delete request, you can see that there are now two cars left in the database:

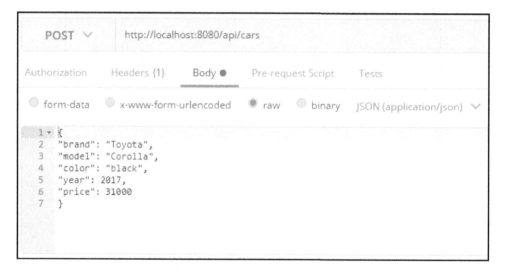

When we want to add a new car to the database, we have to use the POST method, and the link is `http://localhost:8080/api/cars`. The header must contain the **Content-Type** field with the value `Content-Type:application/json`, and the new car object will be embedded in the request body:

```
POST ∨          http://localhost:8080/api/cars

Authorization    Headers (1)    Body ●    Pre-request Script    Tests

  form-data    x-www-form-urlencoded    raw    binary    JSON (application/json) ∨

1 ▾ {
2    "brand": "Toyota",
3    "model": "Corolla",
4    "color": "black",
5    "year": 2017,
6    "price": 31000
7    }
```

The response will send a newly created `car` object back. Now, if you again make a `GET` request to the `http://localhost:8080/api/cars` path, you can see that the new car exists in the database:

To update entities, we have to use the `PATCH` method and the link to the car that we want to update (`http://localhost:8080/api/cars/{id}`). The header must contain the **Content-Type** field with the value `Content-Type:application/json`, and the car object, with edited data, will be given inside the request body. If you are using `PATCH`, you have to send only fields that are updates. If you are using `PUT`, you have to include all fields to request. Let's edit our car that we created in the previous example. We will change the color to white and fill in the register number that we left empty.

We will also link an owner to the car by using the owner field. The content of the owner field is the link to the owner (`http://localhost:8080/api/owners/{id}`). The following screenshot shows the `PATCH` request content:

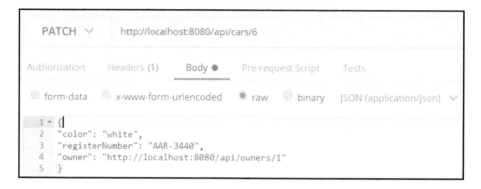

You can see that the car is updated after you fetch all cars by using the `GET` request:

```
GET  ∨        http://localhost:8080/api/cars

Pretty    Raw    Preview    JSON  ∨   ⇒

59                    }
60              },
61 ▾           {
62                  "brand": "Toyota",
63                  "model": "Corolla",
64                  "color": "white",
65                  "registerNumber": "AAR-3440",
66                  "year": 2017,
67                  "price": 31000,
68 ▾               "_links": {
69 ▾                   "self": {
70                         "href": "http://localhost:8080/api/cars/6"
71                     },
72 ▾                   "car": {
73                         "href": "http://localhost:8080/api/cars/6"
74                     },
75 ▾                   "owner": {
76                         "href": "http://localhost:8080/api/cars/6/owner"
77                     }
78                  }
79              }
80          ]
81      },
```

In the previous chapter, we created queries to our repository. These queries can also be included in our service. To include queries, you have to add the @RepositoryRestResource annotation to the repository class. Query parameters are annotated with the @Param annotation. The following source code shows our CarRepository with these annotations:

```
package com.packt.cardatabase.domain;

import java.util.List;

import org.springframework.data.repository.CrudRepository;
import org.springframework.data.repository.query.Param;
import
org.springframework.data.rest.core.annotation.RepositoryRestResource;

@RepositoryRestResource
public interface CarRepository extends CrudRepository <Car, Long> {
  // Fetch cars by brand
  List<Car> findByBrand(@Param("brand") String brand);

  // Fetch cars by color
  List<Car> findByColor(@Param("color") String color);
}
```

Now, when you make a GET request to the http://localhost:8080/api/cars path, you can see that there is a new endpoint called /search. Calling the http://localhost:8080/api/cars/search path returns the following response:

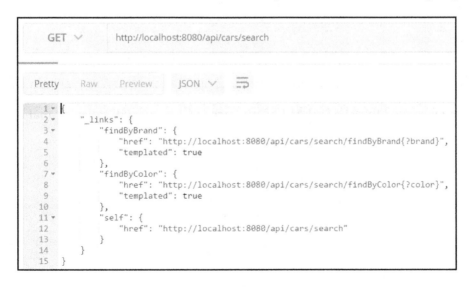

From the response, you can see that both queries are now available in our service. The following URL demonstrates how to fetch cars by brand:

```
http://localhost:8080/api/cars/search/findByBrand?brand=Ford
```

The following screenshot is the output of the preceding URL:

```
GET  ∨        http://localhost:8080/api/cars/search/findByBrand?brand=Ford

Pretty    Raw    Preview    JSON  ∨   ⇥

1 ▾  {
2 ▾      "_embedded": {
3 ▾          "cars": [
4 ▾              {
5                   "brand": "Ford",
6                   "model": "Mustang",
7                   "color": "Red",
8                   "registerNumber": "ADF-1121",
9                   "year": 2017,
10                  "price": 59000,
11 ▾                "_links": {
12 ▾                    "self": {
13                          "href": "http://localhost:8080/api/cars/3"
14                      },
15 ▾                    "car": {
16                          "href": "http://localhost:8080/api/cars/3"
17                      },
18 ▾                    "owner": {
19                          "href": "http://localhost:8080/api/cars/3/owner"
20                      }
21                  }
22              }
23          ]
24      },
```

We have now created the RESTful API to our backend and we will consume that later with our React frontend.

Summary

In this chapter, we created a RESTful web service with Spring Boot. First, we created a controller and one method that returns all cars in JSON format. Next, we used Spring Data REST to get a fully functional web service with all CRUD functionalities. We covered different types of requests that are needed to use CRUD functionalities of the service that we created. Finally, we also included our queries to service.

In the next chapter, we will secure our backend using Spring Security.

Questions

1. What is REST?
2. How can you create a RESTful web service with Spring Boot?
3. How can you fetch items using our RESTful web service?
4. How can you delete items using our RESTful web service?
5. How can you add items using our RESTful web service?
6. How can you update items using our RESTful web service?
7. How can you use queries with our RESTful web service?

Further reading

Pack has other great resources available for learning about Spring Boot RESTful web services. These are as follows:

- *Learning Spring Boot 2.0 – Second Edition*, by Greg L. Turnquist (https://www.packtpub.com/application-development/learning-spring-boot-20-second-edition)
- *Spring Boot – Getting Started* [Integrated Course], by Patrick Cornelissen (https://www.packtpub.com/web-development/spring-boot-getting-started-integrated-course)
- *Building a RESTful Web Service with Spring*, by Ludovic Dewailly (https://www.packtpub.com/web-development/building-restful-web-service-spring)

5
Securing and Testing Your Backend

This chapter explains how to secure and test your Spring Boot backend. Securing your backend is a crucial part of backend development. In the testing part of this chapter we will create some unit tests in relation to our backend. Unit tests make your backend code easier to maintain. We will use the database application that we created in the previous chapter as a starting point.

In this chapter, we will cover the following topics:

- How to secure your Spring Boot backend with Spring Boot
- How to secure your Spring Boot backend with JWT
- How to test your backend

Technical requirements

The Spring Boot application that we created in the previous chapters is required.

The following GitHub link will also be required: `https://github.com/PacktPublishing/Hands-On-Full-Stack-Development-with-Spring-Boot-2-and-React-Second-Edition/tree/master/Chapter05`.

Spring Security

Spring Security (`https://spring.io/projects/spring-security`) provides security services for Java-based web applications. The Spring Security project was started in 2003 and was previously named *The Acegi Security System for Spring*.

By default, Spring Security enables the following features:

- An `AuthenticationManager` bean with an in-memory single user. The username is `user` and the password is printed to the console output.
- Ignored paths for common static resource locations, such as `/css` and `/images`.
- HTTP basic security for all other endpoints.
- Security events published to Spring's `ApplicationEventPublisher`.
- Common low-level features are on by default (HSTS, XSS, CSRF, and so forth).

You can include Spring Security in your application by adding the following dependency to the `pom.xml` file:

```xml
<dependency>
  <groupId>org.springframework.boot</groupId>
  <artifactId>spring-boot-starter-security</artifactId>
</dependency>
```

When you start your application, you can see from the console that Spring Security has created an in-memory user with the username `user`. The user's password can be seen in the console output:

If you make a `GET` request to your API endpoint, you will see that it is now secure, and you will get a `401 Unauthorized` error:

To be able to make a successful GET request, we have to use basic authentication. The following screenshot shows how to do this with Postman. With authentication, we can see that the status is **200 OK** and that the response has been sent:

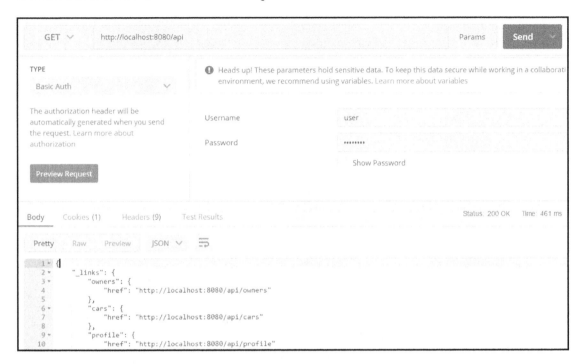

To configure how Spring Security behaves, we have to add a new configuration class that extends WebSecurityConfigurerAdapter. Create a new class called SecurityConfig in your application root package. The following source code shows the structure of the security configuration class. The @Configuration and @EnableWebSecurity annotations switch off the default web security configuration, and we can define our own configuration in this class. Inside the configure(HttpSecurity http) method, we can define which endpoints in our application are secure and which are not. We actually don't need this method yet because we can use the default settings where all the endpoints are secured:

```
package com.packt.cardatabase;

import org.springframework.context.annotation.Configuration;
import
org.springframework.security.config.annotation.web.builders.HttpSecurity;
import
org.springframework.security.config.annotation.web.configuration.EnableWebS
ecurity;
```

```
import
org.springframework.security.config.annotation.web.configuration.WebSecurit
yConfigurerAdapter;

@Configuration
@EnableWebSecurity
public class SecurityConfig extends WebSecurityConfigurerAdapter {
  @Override
  protected void configure(HttpSecurity http) throws Exception {

  }

}
```

We can also add in-memory users to our application by adding
the userDetailsService() method to our SecurityConfig class. The following is the
source code of the method, and it will create an in-memory user with the username
user and the password password:

```
@Bean
@Override
public UserDetailsService userDetailsService() {
    UserDetails user =
        User.withDefaultPasswordEncoder()
            .username("user")
            .password("password")
            .roles("USER")
            .build();

    return new InMemoryUserDetailsManager(user);
}
```

The use of in-memory users is good in the development phase, but the real application
should save the users in the database. To save the users to the database, you have to create
a user entity class and repository. Passwords shouldn't be saved to the database in plain
text format. Spring Security provides multiple hashing algorithms, such as BCrypt, that you
can use to hash passwords. The following steps show you how to implement this:

1. Create a new class called User in the domain package. Activate the domain
   package and right-click it. Select **New** | **Class** from the menu and give the name
   User to a new class. After that, your project structure should look like the
   following screenshot:

2. Annotate the User class with the @Entity annotation. Add the id, username, password, and role class fields. Finally, add the constructors, getters, and setters. We will set all the fields to be nullable, and specify that the username must be unique by using the @Column annotation. Refer to the following User.java source code of the fields and constructors:

```java
package com.packt.cardatabase.domain;

import javax.persistence.Column;
import javax.persistence.Entity;
import javax.persistence.GeneratedValue;
import javax.persistence.GenerationType;
import javax.persistence.Id;

@Entity
public class User {
    @Id
    @GeneratedValue(strategy = GenerationType.IDENTITY)
    @Column(nullable = false, updatable = false)
    private Long id;

    @Column(nullable = false, unique = true)
    private String username;
```

```
@Column(nullable = false)
private String password;

@Column(nullable = false)
private String role;

public User() {
}
public User(String username, String password, String role) {
    super();
    this.username = username;
    this.password = password;
    this.role = role;
}
```

The following is the rest of the User.java source code with the getters and setters:

```
public Long getId() {
    return id;
}

public void setId(Long id) {
    this.id = id;
}

public String getUsername() {
    return username;
}

public void setUsername(String username) {
    this.username = username;
}

public String getPassword() {
    return password;
}

public void setPassword(String password) {
    this.password = password;
}

public String getRole() {
    return role;
}

public void setRole(String role) {
    this.role = role;
```

```
    }
  }
```

3. Create a new class called `UserRepository` in the `domain` package. Activate the `domain` package and right-click it. Select **New** | **Class** from the menu and give the name `UserRepository` to the new class.

4. The source code of the repository class is similar to what we made in the previous chapter, but there is one query method, `findByUsername`, that we need for the steps that follow. Refer to the following `UserRepository` source code:

```
package com.packt.cardatabase.domain;

import org.springframework.data.repository.CrudRepository;
import org.springframework.stereotype.Repository;

@Repository
public interface UserRepository extends CrudRepository<User, Long>
{
    User findByUsername(String username);
}
```

5. Next, we will create a class that implements the `UserDetailsService` interface that's provided by Spring Security. Spring Security uses this for user authentication and authorization. Create a new package in the root package called `service`. Activate the root package and right-click it. Select **New** | **Package** from the menu and give the name `service` to a new package:

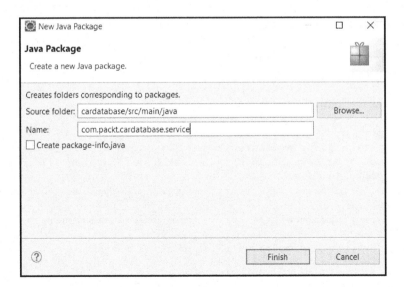

6. Create a new class called `UserDetailServiceImpl` in the `service` package we just created. Now, your project structure should look like the following:

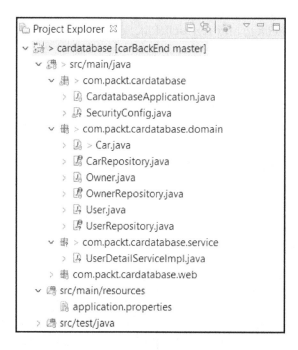

7. We have to inject the `UserRepository` class into the `UserDetailServiceImpl` class because that is needed to fetch the user from the database when Spring Security handles authentication.
   The `loadByUsername` method returns the `UserDetails` object, which is required for authentication. The following is the source code of `UserDetailServiceImpl.java`:

```
package com.packt.cardatabase.service;

import org.springframework.beans.factory.annotation.Autowired;
import org.springframework.security.core.authority.AuthorityUtils;
import org.springframework.security.core.userdetails.UserDetails;
import
org.springframework.security.core.userdetails.UserDetailsService;
import
org.springframework.security.core.userdetails.UsernameNotFoundExcep
tion;
import org.springframework.stereotype.Service;

import com.packt.cardatabase.domain.User;
```

```
import com.packt.cardatabase.domain.UserRepository;

@Service
public class UserDetailServiceImpl implements UserDetailsService {
  @Autowired
  private UserRepository repository;


    @Override
    public UserDetails loadUserByUsername(String username) throws
UsernameNotFoundException
    {
      User currentUser = repository.findByUsername(username);
        UserDetails user = new org.springframework.security.core
          .userdetails.User(username, currentUser.getPassword()
          , true, true, true, true,
AuthorityUtils.createAuthorityList(currentUser.getRole()));
        return user;
    }
}
```

8. In our security configuration class, we have to stipulate that Spring Security should use users from the database instead of in-memory users. Delete the `userDetailsService()` method from the `SecurityConfig` class to disable in-memory users. Add a new `configureGlobal` method to enable users from the database. We should never save the password as plain text to the database. Therefore, we will define a password hashing algorithm in the `configureGlobal` method. In this example, we are using the BCrypt algorithm. This can be easily implemented with the Spring Security `BCryptPasswordEncoder` class. The following is the `SecurityConfig.java` source code. Now, the password must be hashed using BCrypt before it's saved to the database:

```
package com.packt.cardatabase;

import org.springframework.beans.factory.annotation.Autowired;
import org.springframework.context.annotation.Configuration;
import
org.springframework.security.config.annotation.authentication.build
ers.AuthenticationManagerBuilder;
import
org.springframework.security.config.annotation.web.builders.HttpSec
urity;
import
org.springframework.security.config.annotation.web.configuration.En
ableWebSecurity;
```

```
import
org.springframework.security.config.annotation.web.configuration.We
bSecurityConfigurerAdapter;
import
org.springframework.security.crypto.bcrypt.BCryptPasswordEncoder;

import com.packt.cardatabase.service.UserDetailServiceImpl;

@Configuration
@EnableWebSecurity
public class SecurityConfig extends WebSecurityConfigurerAdapter {
  @Autowired
  private UserDetailServiceImpl userDetailsService;

  @Autowired
  public void configureGlobal(AuthenticationManagerBuilder auth)
throws Exception {
    auth.userDetailsService(userDetailsService)
    .passwordEncoder(new BCryptPasswordEncoder());
  }
}
```

9. Finally, we can save a couple of test users to the database in our `CommandLineRunner`. Open the `CardatabaseApplication.java` file and add the following code at the beginning of the class to inject `UserRepository` into the `main` class:

```
@Autowired
private UserRepository urepository;
```

10. Save the users to the database with hashed passwords. You can use any BCrypt calculator on the internet to do so:

```
@Bean
CommandLineRunner runner() {
  return args -> {
    Owner owner1 = new Owner("John" , "Johnson");
    Owner owner2 = new Owner("Mary" , "Robinson");
    orepository.save(owner1);
    orepository.save(owner2);
    repository.save(new Car("Ford", "Mustang", "Red", "ADF-1121",
      2017, 59000, owner1));
    repository.save(new Car("Nissan", "Leaf", "White", "SSJ-3002",
      2014, 29000, owner2));
    repository.save(new Car("Toyota", "Prius", "Silver", "KKO-0212",
      2018, 39000, owner2));
    // username: user password: user
```

```
urepository.save(new User("user",
"$2a$04$1.YhMIgNX/8TkCKGFUONWO1waedKhQ5KrnB30fl0Q01QKqmzLf.Zi",
"USER"));
// username: admin password: admin
urepository.save(new User("admin",
"$2a$04$KNLUwOWHVQZVpXyMBNc7JOzbLiBjb9Tk9bP7KNcPI12ICuvzXQQKG",
"ADMIN"));
};
}
```

After running your application, you will see that there is now a `user` table in the database and that two user records are saved:

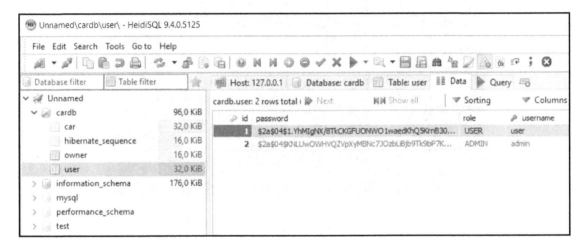

Now, you will get a `401 Unauthorized` error if you try to send a `GET` request to the `/api` endpoint without authentication. You should authenticate to be able to send a successful request. The difference, when compared with the previous example, is that we are using the users from the database to authenticate.

You can see a `GET` request to the `/api` endpoint using the `admin` user in the following screenshot:

```
root@HHMX4717: ~
root@HHMX4717:~# curl http://localhost:8080/api -u admin
Enter host password for user 'admin':
{
  "_links" : {
    "owners" : {
      "href" : "http://localhost:8080/api/owners"
    },
    "users" : {
      "href" : "http://localhost:8080/api/users"
    },
    "cars" : {
      "href" : "http://localhost:8080/api/cars"
    },
    "profile" : {
      "href" : "http://localhost:8080/api/profile"
    }
  }
}root@HHMX4717:~#
```

Next, we will start to implement authentication using JSON web tokens.

Securing your backend using JWT

In the previous section, we covered how to use basic authentication with the RESTful web service. This method cannot be used when we develop our own frontend with React, so we are going to use **JSON Web Token (JWT)** authentication instead. JWT is a compact way to implement authentication in modern web applications. JWT is really small in size and can therefore be sent in the URL, in the `POST` parameter, or inside the header. It also contains all the necessary information pertaining to the user.

The JSON web token contains three different parts, separated by dots:

- The first part is the header that defines the type of the token and the hashing algorithm.
- The second part is the payload that, typically, in the case of authentication, contains information pertaining to the user.

- The third part is the signature that is used to verify that the token hasn't been changed along the way. The following is an example of a JWT token:

```
eyJhbGciOiJIUzI1NiJ9.
eyJzdWIiOiJKb2UifD.
ipevRNuRP6HflG8cFKnmUPtypruRC4fc1DWtoLL62SY
```

The following diagram shows the main idea of the JWT authentication process:

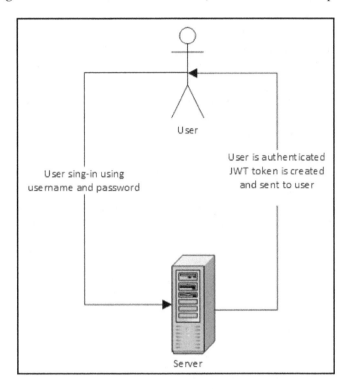

After successful authentication, the requests sent by the user should always contain the JWT token that was received in the authentication.

We will use the Java JWT library (`https://github.com/jwtk/jjwt`), which is the JWT library for Java and Android. Therefore, we have to add the following dependency to the `pom.xml` file. The JWT library is used for creating and parsing JWT tokens:

```xml
<dependency>
  <groupId>io.jsonwebtoken</groupId>
  <artifactId>jjwt</artifactId>
  <version>0.9.1</version>
</dependency>
```

If you are using Java version 9 or greater, add the following dependency to the `pom.xml` file:

```
<dependency>
    <groupId>javax.xml.bind</groupId>
    <artifactId>jaxb-api</artifactId>
</dependency>
```

The following steps demonstrate how to enable JWT authentication in our backend:

1. Create a new class called `AuthenticationService` in the `service` package. At the beginning of the class, we will define a few constants—EXPIRATIONTIME defines the expiration time of the token in milliseconds, while SIGNINGKEY is an algorithm-specific signing key that's used to digitally sign the JWT. You should use a base64-encoded string to do this. PREFIX defines the prefix of the token, and the `Bearer` schema is typically used. The `addToken` method creates the token and adds it to the request's `Authorization` header. The signing key is encoded using the SHA-512 algorithm. The method also adds `Access-Control-Expose-Headers` to the header with the `Authorization` value. This is needed because we are unable to access the `Authorization` header through a JavaScript frontend by default. The `getAuthentication` method gets the token from the response `Authorization` header using the `parser()` method provided by the `jjwt` library. The whole `AuthenticationService` source code can be seen here:

```java
package com.packt.cardatabase.service;

import io.jsonwebtoken.Jwts;
import io.jsonwebtoken.SignatureAlgorithm;
import
org.springframework.security.authentication.UsernamePasswordAuthent
icationToken;
import org.springframework.security.core.Authentication;

import javax.servlet.http.HttpServletRequest;
import javax.servlet.http.HttpServletResponse;
import java.util.Date;

import static java.util.Collections.emptyList;

public class AuthenticationService {
  static final long EXPIRATIONTIME = 864_000_00; // 1 day in
milliseconds
  static final String SIGNINGKEY = "SecretKey";
  static final String PREFIX = "Bearer";
```

```
    // Add token to Authorization header
    static public void addToken(HttpServletResponse res, String
username) {
        String JwtToken = Jwts.builder().setSubject(username)
            .setExpiration(new Date(System.currentTimeMillis()
                + EXPIRATIONTIME))
            .signWith(SignatureAlgorithm.HS512, SIGNINGKEY)
            .compact();
        res.addHeader("Authorization", PREFIX + " " + JwtToken);
        res.addHeader("Access-Control-Expose-Headers", "Authorization");
    }

    // Get token from Authorization header
    static public Authentication getAuthentication(HttpServletRequest
request) {
        String token = request.getHeader("Authorization");
        if (token != null) {
          String user = Jwts.parser()
              .setSigningKey(SIGNINGKEY)
              .parseClaimsJws(token.replace(PREFIX, ""))
              .getBody()
              .getSubject();

          if (user != null)
            return new UsernamePasswordAuthenticationToken(user, null,
                emptyList());
        }
        return null;
    }
}
```

2. Next, we will add a new simple POJO class to keep credentials for authentication. Create a new class called `AccountCredentials` in the `domain` package. The class has two fields—`username` and `password`. The following is the source code of the class. This class doesn't have the `@Entity` annotation because we don't have to save credentials to the database:

```
package com.packt.cardatabase.domain;

public class AccountCredentials {
  private String username;
  private String password;
  public String getUsername() {
    return username;
  }
  public void setUsername(String username) {
    this.username = username;
```

```
    }
    public String getPassword() {
      return password;
    }
    public void setPassword(String password) {
      this.password = password;
    }
  }
```

3. We will use filter classes for login and authentication. Create a new class called `LoginFilter` in the root package that handles `POST` requests to the `/login` endpoint. The `LoginFilter` class extends Spring Security's `AbstractAuthenticationProcessingFilter` interface, which requires that you set the `authenticationManager` property. Authentication is performed by the `attemptAuthentication` method. If authentication is successful, the `succesfulAuthentication` method is executed. This method will then call the `addToken` method in our service class, and the token will be added to the `Authorization` header:

```
package com.packt.cardatabase;

import java.io.IOException;
import java.util.Collections;

import javax.servlet.FilterChain;
import javax.servlet.ServletException;
import javax.servlet.http.HttpServletRequest;
import javax.servlet.http.HttpServletResponse;

import
org.springframework.security.authentication.AuthenticationManager;
import
org.springframework.security.authentication.UsernamePasswordAuthent
icationToken;
import org.springframework.security.core.Authentication;
import org.springframework.security.core.AuthenticationException;
import
org.springframework.security.web.authentication.AbstractAuthenticat
ionProcessingFilter;
import
org.springframework.security.web.util.matcher.AntPathRequestMatcher
;

import com.fasterxml.jackson.databind.ObjectMapper;
import com.packt.cardatabase.domain.AccountCredentials;
import com.packt.cardatabase.service.AuthenticationService;
```

```
public class LoginFilter extends
AbstractAuthenticationProcessingFilter {

  public LoginFilter(String url, AuthenticationManager authManager)
{
    super(new AntPathRequestMatcher(url));
    setAuthenticationManager(authManager);
  }

  @Override
  public Authentication attemptAuthentication(
  HttpServletRequest req, HttpServletResponse res)
      throws AuthenticationException, IOException, ServletException
{
  AccountCredentials creds = new ObjectMapper()
        .readValue(req.getInputStream(), AccountCredentials.class);
  return getAuthenticationManager().authenticate(
        new UsernamePasswordAuthenticationToken(
            creds.getUsername(),
            creds.getPassword(),
            Collections.emptyList()
        )
    );
  }

  @Override
  protected void successfulAuthentication(
      HttpServletRequest req,
      HttpServletResponse res, FilterChain chain,
      Authentication auth) throws IOException, ServletException {
    AuthenticationService.addToken(res, auth.getName());
  }
}
```

4. Create a new class called `AuthenticationFilter` in the root package. The class extends `GenericFilterBean`, which is a generic superclass for any type of filter. This class will handle authentication in all other endpoints, except `/login`. `AuthenticationFilter` uses the `getAuthentication` method from our service class to get a token from the request `Authorization` header:

```
package com.packt.cardatabase;

import java.io.IOException;

import javax.servlet.FilterChain;
import javax.servlet.ServletException;
import javax.servlet.ServletRequest;
```

```
import javax.servlet.ServletResponse;
import javax.servlet.http.HttpServletRequest;

import org.springframework.security.core.Authentication;
import
org.springframework.security.core.context.SecurityContextHolder;
import org.springframework.web.filter.GenericFilterBean;

import com.packt.cardatabase.service.AuthenticationService;

public class AuthenticationFilter extends GenericFilterBean {
  @Override
  public void doFilter(ServletRequest request, ServletResponse
response, FilterChain filterChain) throws IOException,
ServletException {
    Authentication authentication =
AuthenticationService.getAuthentication((HttpServletRequest)request
);
    SecurityContextHolder.getContext().
      setAuthentication(authentication);
    filterChain.doFilter(request, response);
  }
}
```

5. Finally, we have to make changes to our `SecurityConfig` class's `configure` method. There, we stipulate that the `POST` method request to the `/login` endpoint is allowed without authentication and that requests to all other endpoints require authentication. We also define the filters to be used in the `/login` and other endpoints by using the `addFilterBefore` method:

```
//SecurityConfig.java
@Override
  protected void configure(HttpSecurity http) throws Exception {
    http.csrf().disable().cors().and().authorizeRequests()
      .antMatchers(HttpMethod.POST, "/login").permitAll()
        .anyRequest().authenticated()
        .and()
        // Filter for the api/login requests
        .addFilterBefore(new LoginFilter("/login",
        authenticationManager()),
              UsernamePasswordAuthenticationFilter.class)
        // Filter for other requests to check JWT in header
        .addFilterBefore(new AuthenticationFilter(),
              UsernamePasswordAuthenticationFilter.class);
    }
```

6. We will also add a **CORS** (short for **Cross-Origin Resource Sharing**) filter in our security configuration class. This is needed for the frontend, which is sending requests from the other origin. The CORS filter intercepts requests, and if these are identified as cross-origin, it adds proper headers to the request. For that, we will use Spring Security's `CorsConfigurationSource` interface. In this example, we will allow all HTTP methods and headers (using "*"). You can define the list of permissible origins, methods, and headers here if you require a more finely graded definition. Add the following source code to your `SecurityConfig` class to enable the CORS filter:

```java
// SecurityConfig.java
@Bean
  CorsConfigurationSource corsConfigurationSource() {
      UrlBasedCorsConfigurationSource source =
          new UrlBasedCorsConfigurationSource();
      CorsConfiguration config = new CorsConfiguration();
      config.setAllowedOrigins(Arrays.asList("*"));
      config.setAllowedMethods(Arrays.asList("*"));
      config.setAllowedHeaders(Arrays.asList("*"));
      config.setAllowCredentials(true);
      config.applyPermitDefaultValues();
      source.registerCorsConfiguration("/**", config);
      return source;
}
```

Now, after we run the application, we can call the `/login` endpoint with the `POST` method and, in the case of a successful login, we will receive a JWT token in the `Authorization` header:

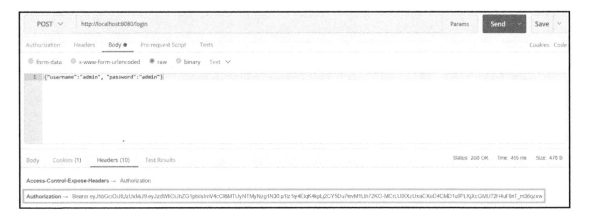

Following a successful login, we can call the other RESTful service endpoints by sending the JWT token that was received from the login in the `Authorization` header. Refer to the example in the following screenshot:

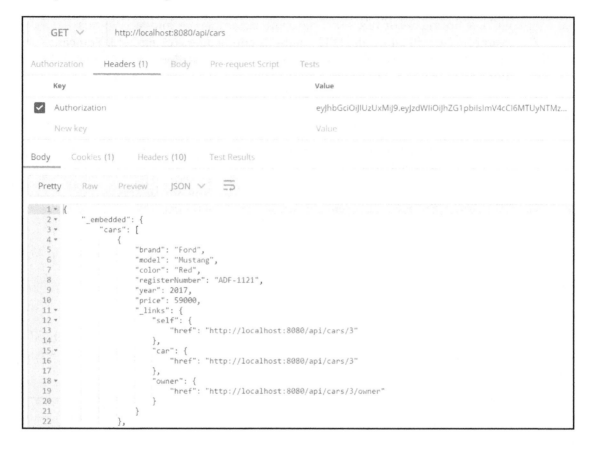

Now, all the functionalities that are required have been implemented to our backend. Next, we will continue with backend unit testing.

Testing in Spring Boot

The Spring Boot test starter package is added to `pom.xml` by Spring Initializr when we create our project. This is added automatically without any selection in the **Spring Initializr** page:

```xml
<dependency>
  <groupId>org.springframework.boot</groupId>
  <artifactId>spring-boot-starter-test</artifactId>
  <scope>test</scope>
</dependency>
```

The Spring Boot test starter provides lots of handy libraries for testing, such as JUnit, Mockito, and AssertJ. If you take a look, your project structure already has its own package created for test classes:

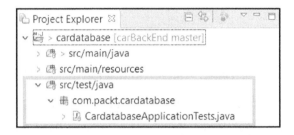

By default, Spring Boot uses an in-memory database for testing. We are now using MariaDB, but H2 can also be used for testing if we add the following dependency to the `pom.xml` file. The scope defines that the H2 database will only be used for running tests; otherwise, the application will use the MariaDB database:

```xml
<dependency>
    <groupId>com.h2database</groupId>
    <artifactId>h2</artifactId>
    <scope>test</scope>
</dependency>
```

If you also want to use the default database for testing, you can use the `@AutoConfigureTestDatabase` annotation.

Creating unit tests

For unit testing, we are using a JUnit, which is a popular Java-based unit testing library. The following source code shows the example skeleton of the Spring Boot test class. The `@SpringBootTest` annotation specifies that the class is a regular test class that runs Spring Boot-based tests. The `@Test` annotation before the method specifies to JUnit that the method can be run as a test case. The `@RunWith(SpringRunner.class)` annotation provides Spring's `ApplicationContext` and gets beans injected into your test instance:

```
@RunWith(SpringRunner.class)
@SpringBootTest
public class MyTestsClass {

  @Test
  public void testMethod() {
    ...
  }

}
```

First, we will create our first test case, which will test the major functionality of our application before we create any formal test cases. Open the `CardatabaseApplicationTest` test class that has already been made for your application. There is one test method called `contextLoads` here, and is where we will add the test. The following test checks that the instance of the controller was created and injected successfully:

```
package com.packt.cardatabase;

import static org.assertj.core.api.Assertions.assertThat;

import org.junit.Test;
import org.junit.runner.RunWith;
import org.springframework.beans.factory.annotation.Autowired;
import org.springframework.boot.test.context.SpringBootTest;
import org.springframework.test.context.junit4.SpringRunner;

import com.packt.cardatabase.web.CarController;

@RunWith(SpringRunner.class)
@SpringBootTest
public class CardatabaseApplicationTests {
  @Autowired
  private CarController controller;

  @Test
```

```
  public void contextLoads() {
    assertThat(controller).isNotNull();
  }

}
```

To run tests in Eclipse, activate the test class in the **Project Explorer** and right-click. Select **Run As | JUnit test** from the menu. You should now see the **JUnit** tab in the lower part of the Eclipse workbench. The test results are shown in this tab and the test case has been passed:

Next, we will create unit tests for our car repository to test CRUD operations. Create a new class called `CarRepositoryTest` in the root test package. Instead of the `@SpringBootTest` annotation, `@DataJpaTest` can be used if the test focuses only on JPA components. When using this annotation, the H2 database, Hibernate, and Spring Data are configured automatically for testing. SQL logging is also turned on. The tests are transactional by default and roll back at the end of the test case. `TestEntityManager` is used to handle the persist entities and is designed to be used in testing. You can see the source code of the JPA test class skeleton in the following code snippet:

```
package com.packt.cardatabase;

import static org.assertj.core.api.Assertions.assertThat;

import org.junit.Test;
import org.junit.runner.RunWith;
import org.springframework.beans.factory.annotation.Autowired;
import org.springframework.boot.test.autoconfigure.orm.jpa.DataJpaTest;
import
org.springframework.boot.test.autoconfigure.orm.jpa.TestEntityManager;
import org.springframework.test.context.junit4.SpringRunner;

import com.packt.cardatabase.domain.Car;
import com.packt.cardatabase.domain.CarRepository;

@RunWith(SpringRunner.class)
@DataJpaTest
public class CarRepositoryTest {
  @Autowired
```

```
    private TestEntityManager entityManager;
    @Autowired
    private CarRepository repository;
      // Test cases..
  }
```

We will add out first test case to test the addition of a new car to the database. A new car object is created and saved to the database with the persistAndFlush method provided by TestEntityManager. Then, we check that the car ID cannot be null if it is saved successfully. The following source code shows the test case method. Add the following method code to your CarRepositoryTest class:

```
@Test
public void saveCar() {
  Car car = new Car("Tesla", "Model X", "White", "ABC-1234",
      2017, 86000);
  entityManager.persistAndFlush(car);
  assertThat(car.getId()).isNotNull();
}
```

The second test case will test the deletion of cars from the database. A new car object is created and saved to the database. Then, all cars are deleted from the database, and finally, the findAll() query method should return an empty list. The following source code shows the test case method. Add the following method code to your CarRepositoryTest class:

```
@Test
public void deleteCars() {
  entityManager.persistAndFlush(new Car("Tesla", "Model X", "White",
      "ABC-1234", 2017, 86000));
  entityManager.persistAndFlush(new Car("Mini", "Cooper", "Yellow",
      "BWS-3007", 2015, 24500));
  repository.deleteAll();
  assertThat(repository.findAll()).isEmpty();
}
```

Run the test cases and check the Eclipse **JUnit** tab to find out whether the tests passed:

Next, we will demonstrate how to test your RESTful web service JWT authentication functionality. To test the controllers or any endpoint that is exposed, we can use a MockMvc object. By using the MockMvc object, the server is not started, but the tests are performed in the layer where Spring handles HTTP requests, and therefore it mocks the real situation. MockMvc provides the perform method to send these requests. To test authentication, we have to add credentials to the request body. We will perform two requests—the first has the correct credentials, and we check that the status is **OK**. The second request contains incorrect credentials and we check that we get a 4XX HTTP error:

```java
package com.packt.cardatabase;

import static
org.springframework.test.web.servlet.request.MockMvcRequestBuilders.post;
import static
org.springframework.test.web.servlet.result.MockMvcResultHandlers.print;
import static
org.springframework.test.web.servlet.result.MockMvcResultMatchers.status;

import org.junit.Test;
import org.junit.runner.RunWith;
import org.springframework.beans.factory.annotation.Autowired;
import
org.springframework.boot.test.autoconfigure.web.servlet.AutoConfigureMockMvc;
import org.springframework.boot.test.context.SpringBootTest;

import org.springframework.test.context.junit4.SpringRunner;
import org.springframework.test.web.servlet.MockMvc;

@RunWith(SpringRunner.class)
@SpringBootTest
@AutoConfigureMockMvc
public class CarRestTest {
  @Autowired
    private MockMvc mockMvc;
  @Test
  public void testAuthentication() throws Exception {
```

```
    // Testing authentication with correct credentials
        this.mockMvc.perform(post("/login")
            .content("{\"username\":\"admin\", \"password\":\"admin\"}")).
            andDo(print()).andExpect(status().isOk());

    // Testing authentication with wrong credentials
        this.mockMvc.perform(post("/login")
            .content("{\"username\":\"admin\", \"password\":\"wrongpwd\"}")).
            andDo(print()).andExpect(status().is4xxClientError());
    }

}
```

Now, when we run the authentication tests, we will see that the test passed:

At this point, we have covered the basics of testing in the Spring Boot application, and you have gained the knowledge that's required to implement more test cases for your application.

Summary

In this chapter, we focused on securing and testing the Spring Boot backend. First, securing was done with Spring Security. The frontend will be developed with React in upcoming chapters; therefore, we implemented JWT authentication, which is a lightweight authentication method suitable for our needs.

We also covered the basics of testing a Spring Boot application. We used JUnit for unit testing and implemented test cases for JPA and RESTful web service authentication.

In the next chapter, we will set up the environment and tools related to frontend development.

Questions

1. What is Spring Security?
2. How can you secure your backend with Spring Boot?
3. What is JWT?
4. How can you secure your backend with JWT?
5. How can you create unit tests with Spring Boot?
6. How can you run and check the results of unit tests?

Further reading

Packt has other great resources available so that you can learn about Spring Security and testing. These are as follows:

- *Spring Security – Third Edition*, by Peter Mularien, Mick Knutson and et al (https://www.packtpub.com/application-development/spring-security-third-edition)
- *Mastering Software Testing with JUnit 5*, by Boni García (https://www.packtpub.com/web-development/mastering-software-testing-junit-5)

Section 2: Frontend Programming with React

The reader will be familiar with the basics of React. This section focuses on how to consume a RESTful web service with React and how to test the frontend.

This section covers the following chapters:

6
Setting Up the Environment and Tools - Frontend

This chapter describes the development environment and tools that are needed for React, and is required so that you can start frontend development. In this chapter, we will create a simple starter React app by using the *Create React App* starter kit that's developed by Facebook.

In this chapter, we will cover the following topics:

- Installing Node.js
- Installing VS Code
- VS Code extensions
- Creating a React.js app using `create-react-app`
- Running a React app

Technical requirements

In this book, we are using the Windows OS, but all the tools we use are available for Linux and macOS as well.

The following GitHub link will also be required: `https://github.com/PacktPublishing/Hands-On-Full-Stack-Development-with-Spring-Boot-2-and-React-Second-Edition/tree/master/Chapter06`.

Installing Node.js

Node.js is an open source, JavaScript-based server-side environment. Node.js is available for multiple operating systems, such as Windows, macOS, and Linux, and is required to develop React apps.

The Node.js installation package can be found at https://nodejs.org/en/download/. Download the latest **Long Term Support** (**LTS**) version for your operating system. In this book, we are using the Windows 10 operating system, and you can get the Node.js MSI installer for it, which makes installation really straightforward. When you execute the installer, you will go through the installation wizard, and you can do so using the default settings:

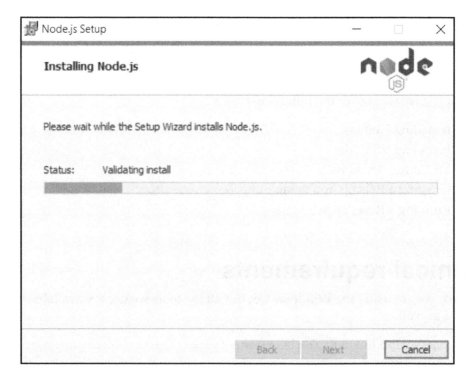

Once the installation is complete, we can check that everything proceeded correctly. Open PowerShell, or whatever terminal you are using, and type the following commands:

```
node -v
npm -v
```

These commands should show you the installed versions of Node.js and Npm:

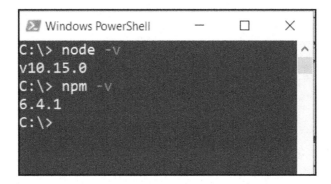

Npm comes with the Node.js installation, and is a package manager for JavaScript. We will use this a lot in the following chapters when we install different node modules on our React app. There is also another package manager called Yarn that you can use as well.

Installing VS Code

Visual Studio Code (VS Code) is an open source code editor for multiple programming languages. VS Code was developed by Microsoft. There are a lot of different code editors available, such as Atom and Brackets, and you can use something other than VS Code if you are familiar with it. VS Code is available for Windows, macOS, and Linux, and you can download it from https://code.visualstudio.com/.

Installation for Windows is done with the MSI installer, and you can execute the installation with default settings. The following screenshot shows the workbench of VS Code. On the left-hand side is the activity bar, which you can use to navigate between different views. Next to the activity bar is a sidebar, that contains different views, such as the project file explorer.

The editor takes up the rest of the workbench:

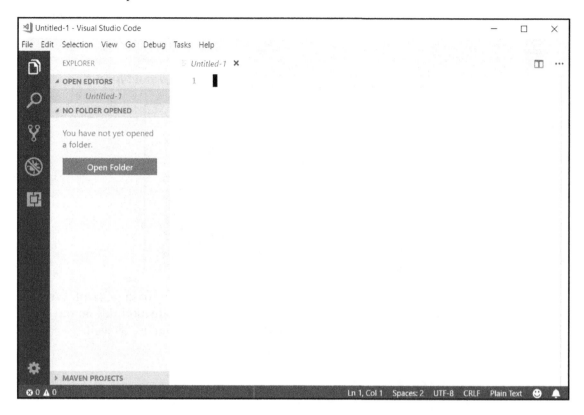

VS Code also has an integrated terminal that you can use to create and run React apps. The terminal can be found in the **View** | **Integrated Terminal** menu. You will use this in later chapters when we create more React apps.

VS Code extension

There are a lot of extensions available for different programming languages and frameworks. If you open **Extension Manager** from the activity bar, you can search for different extensions. One really handy extension for React development is **Reactjs code snippets**, which we recommend installing. It has multiple code snippets available for the React.js app, which makes your development process faster. We will show you how to use that extension later:

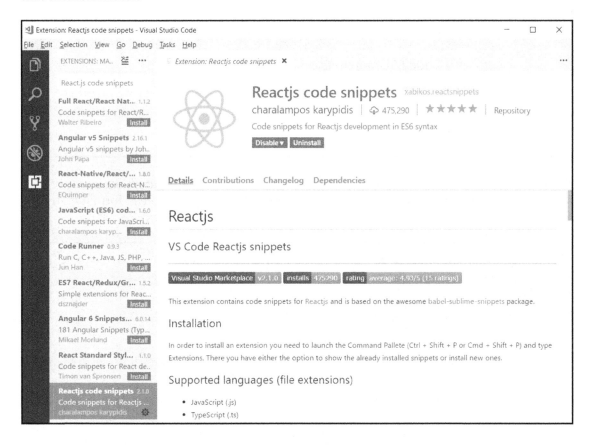

The **ESLint** extension helps you find typos and syntax errors quickly and makes formatting the source code easier:

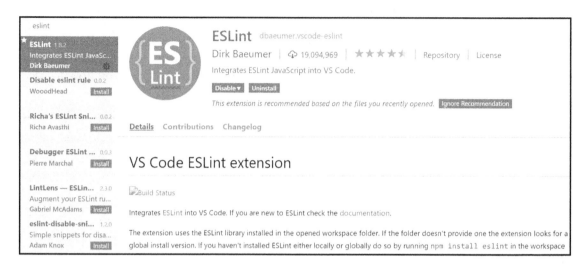

Prettier is a code formatter. With the Prettier extension, you can get automatic code formatting. You can also set this from the VS Code settings so that you can format code automatically after saving your code:

These are just a few examples of the great extensions you can get for VS Code.

Creating and running a React app

Now that we have Node.js and the code editor installed, we are ready to create our first React.js app. We are using Facebook's `create-react-app` command (`https://github.com/facebook/create-react-app`) for this. Here are the steps you need to follow in order to make your first app:

1. Open PowerShell or the Command Prompt tool and type the following command:

   ```
   npx create-react-app myapp
   ```

   This command creates a React app named `myapp`. Npx is the `npm` package runner and, when you're using it, you don't have to install the package before running it:

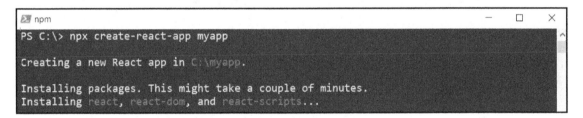

2. Once the app has been created, move it into your `app` folder:

   ```
   cd myapp
   ```

3. Then, we can run the app with the following command. This command runs the app in port `3000` and opens the app in a browser:

   ```
   npm start
   ```

4. Now, your app is running, and you should see the following page in your browser. The `npm start` command starts the app in development mode:

You can stop the development server by pressing *Ctrl + C* in PowerShell.

To build a minified version of your app for production, you can use the `npm run build` command, which builds your app in the `build` folder.

Modifying a React app

Open your React app folder with VS Code by selecting **File** | **Open folder**. You should see the app's structure in the file explorer. The most important folder in this phase is the `src` folder, which contains the JavaScript source codes:

You can also open VS Code by typing the `code .` command into the terminal. This command opens VS Code and the folder where you are located.

Open the `App.js` file from the `src` folder in the code editor. Remove the line that is shown in the following screenshot and save the file. You don't need to know anything else about this file at the moment. We will go deeper into this topic in the next chapter:

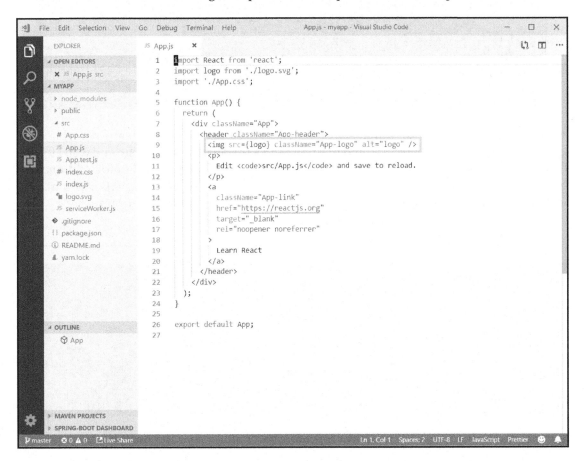

Now, if you look at the browser, you should immediately see that the image has disappeared from the page:

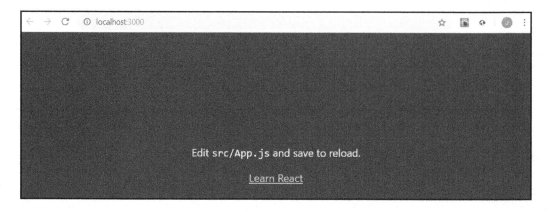

To debug React apps, we should also install React developer tools, which are available for Chrome or Firefox browsers. Chrome plugins can be installed from the chrome web store (`https://chrome.google.com/webstore/category/extensions`), while Firefox add-ons can be installed from the Firefox add-ons site (`https://addons.mozilla.org`). After you have installed the React developer tools, you should see a new **React** tab in your browser's developer tools once you navigate to your React app:

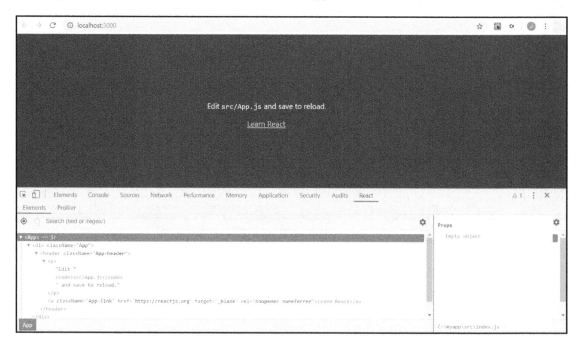

The preceding screenshot shows the developer tools in the Chrome browser.

Summary

In this chapter, we installed everything that is needed to embark on our frontend development with React.js. First, we installed Node.js and the VS Code editor. Then, we used the `create-react-app` starter kit to create our first React.js app. Finally, we ran the app and demonstrated how to modify it. This is just an overview of the app's structure and modification, and we will continue this in the following chapters.

In the next chapter, we will familiarize ourselves with the basics of React programming. In JavaScript, we will be using ES6 syntax because it provides several features that makes coding cleaner.

Questions

1. What is Node.js and Npm?
2. How do you install Node.js?
3. What is VS Code?
4. How do you install VS Code?
5. How do you create a React.js app with `create-react-app`?
6. How do you run a React.js app?
7. How do you make basic modifications to your app?

Further reading

Packt has other great resources available for learning about React. These are as follows:

- *Getting Started with React*, by Doel Sengupta, Manu Singhal, Et al (`https://www.packtpub.com/web-development/getting-started-react`)
- *React 16 Tooling*, by Adam Boduch (`https://www.packtpub.com/web-development/react-16-tooling`)

7
Getting Started with React

This chapter describes the basics of React programming. We will cover the skills that are required to create basic functionalities for the React frontend. In JavaScript, we use the ES6 syntax because it provides many features that make coding cleaner.

In this chapter, we will look at the following topics:

- How to create React components
- Useful ES6 features
- What JSX is
- How to use state and props in components
- Stateless components
- React hooks
- How to handle events and forms in React

Technical requirements

In this book, we will be using the Windows OS, but all of the tools can be used with Linux and macOS as well. For our work with React hooks, React version 16.8 or higher will be required.

You can find more resources at the GitHub link at `https://github.com/PacktPublishing/Hands-On-Full-Stack-Development-with-Spring-Boot-2-and-React-Second-Edition/tree/master/Chapter07`.

Basic React components

According to Facebook, Inc., React is a JavaScript library for user interfaces. Since version 15, React has been developed under the MIT license. React is component-based and the components are independent and reusable. The components are the basic building blocks of React. When you start to develop a UI with React, it is good to start by creating mock interfaces. That way, it will be easy to identify what kind of components you have to create and how they interact.

From the following screenshot of the mock, we can see how the UI can be split into components. In this case, there will be an application root component, a search bar component, a table component, and a table row component:

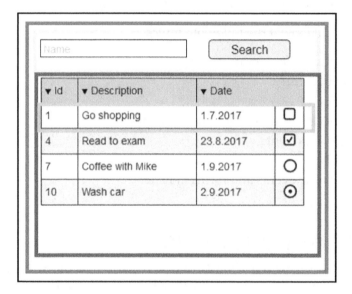

The components can then be arranged in the following tree hierarchy. The important thing to understand with React is that the dataflow is going from the parent component to the child:

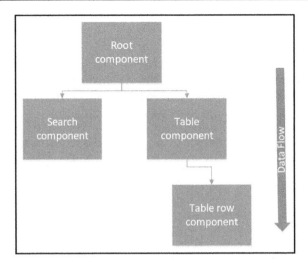

React uses the **virtual DOM (VDOM)** for selective re-rendering of the UI, which makes it more cost effective. The VDOM is a lightweight copy of the DOM, and manipulation of the VDOM is much faster than it is with the real DOM. After the VDOM is updated, React compares it to a snapshot that was taken from the VDOM before updates were run. After the comparison, React will know which parts have been changed, and only these parts will be updated to the real DOM.

The React component can be defined by using a JavaScript function or the ES6 JavaScript class. We will go more deeply into ES6 in the next section. The following is a simple component source code that renders the Hello World text. The first code block uses the JavaScript function:

```
// Using JavaScript function
function Hello() {
  return <h1>Hello World</h1>;
}
```

The following code block uses the ES6 function to create a component:

```
// Using ES6 arrow function
const Hello = () => {
  return <h1>Hello World</h1>;
}
```

The following code uses the class to create a component:

```
// Using ES6 class
class Hello extends React.Component {
  render() {
```

```
    return <h1>Hello World</h1>;
  }
}
```

The component that was implemented using the class contains the required `render()` method. This method shows and updates the rendered output of the component. The name of the user-defined component should start with a capital letter.

Let's make changes to our component's `render` method and add a new header element to it, as follows:

```
function App extends Component {
  render() {
    return (
      <h1>Hello World!</h1>
      <h2>From my first React app</h2>
    );
  }
}
```

When you run the app, you get the `Adjacent JSX elements must be wrapped in an enclosing tag` error. To fix this error, we have to wrap the headers in one element, such as `div`; since React version 16.2, we can also use `Fragments`, which look like empty JSX tags, as shown in the following code:

```
// Wrap headers in div
class App extends Component {
  render() {
    return (
      <div>
        <h1>Hello World!</h1>
        <h2>From my first React app</h2>
      </div>
    );
  }
}

// Or using fragments
class App extends Component {
  render() {
    return (
      <>
        <h1>Hello World!</h1>
        <h2>From my first React app</h2>
      </>
    );
  }
```

}

Let's look more carefully at the first React app that we created in Chapter 6, *Setting Up the Environment and Tools – Frontend*, using `create-react-app`. The source code of the `index.js` file in the root folder appears as follows:

```
import React from 'react';
import ReactDOM from 'react-dom';
import './index.css';
import App from './App';
import * as serviceWorker from './serviceWorker';

ReactDOM.render(<App />, document.getElementById('root'));
serviceWorker.unregister();
```

At the beginning of the file, there are `import` statements that load components or assets to our file. For example, the second line imports the `react-dom` package from the `node_modules` folder, and the fourth line imports the `App` component (the `App.js` file in the root folder). The third line imports the `index.css` style sheet that is in the same folder as the `index.js` file. The `react-dom` package provides DOM-specific methods for us. To render the React component to the DOM, we can use the `render` method from the `react-dom` package.

The first argument is the component that will be rendered, and the second argument is the element or container in which the component will be rendered. In this case, the `root` element is `<div id="root"></div>`, which can be found in the `index.html` file inside the `public` folder. Look at the following `index.html` file:

```
<!DOCTYPE html>
<html lang="en">
  <head>
    <meta charset="utf-8" />
    <link rel="shortcut icon" href="%PUBLIC_URL%/favicon.ico" />
    <meta name="viewport" content="width=device-width, initial-scale=1" />
    <meta name="theme-color" content="#000000" />
    <link rel="manifest" href="%PUBLIC_URL%/manifest.json" />
    <title>React App</title>
  </head>
  <body>
    <noscript>You need to enable JavaScript to run this app.</noscript>
    <div id="root"></div>
  </body>
</html>
```

The following source code shows the `App.js` component from our first React app. You can see that `import` also applies to assets, such as images and style sheets. At the end of the source code, there is an `export` statement that exports the component, and it can be made available to other components by using `import`. There can be only one default `export` per file, but there can be multiple named exports:

```
import React from 'react';
import logo from './logo.svg';
import './App.css';

function App() {
  return (
    <div className="App">
      <header className="App-header">
        <img src={logo} className="App-logo" alt="logo" />
        <p>
          Edit <code>src/App.js</code> and save to reload.
        </p>
        <a
          className="App-link"
          href="https://reactjs.org"
          target="_blank"
          rel="noopener noreferrer"
        >
          Learn React
        </a>
      </header>
    </div>
  );
}

export default App;
```

The following example shows how to import default and named exports:

```
import React from 'react' // Import default value
import { Component } from 'react' // Import named value
```

The exports look like the following:

```
export default React // Default export
export {Component} // Named export
```

Now that we have covered the basic React components, let's take a look at the basic features of ES6.

Basics of ES6

ES6 (short for **ECMAScript 2015**) was released in 2015, and it introduced a lot of new features. ECMAScript is a standardized scripting language, and JavaScript is one implementation of it. In this section, we will go through the most important features released in ES6 that we will be using in the following sections.

Understanding constants

Constants, or immutable variables, can be defined by using a `const` keyword, as shown in the following code. When using the `const` keyword, the variable content cannot be reassigned:

```
const PI = 3.14159;
```

The scope of `const` is block scoped, which is the same as the scope for `let`. This means that the `const` variable can only be used inside the block in which it is defined. In practice, the block is the area between curly brackets { }. The following sample code shows how the scope works:

```
var count = 10;
if(count > 5) {
  const total = count * 2;
  console.log(total); // Prints 20 to console
}
console.log(total); // Error, outside the scope
```

The second `console.log` statement gives an error because we are trying to use the `total` variable outside the scope.

The following example demonstrates what happens when `const` is an object or array:

```
const myObj = {foo : 3};
myObj.foo = 5; // This is ok
```

When `const` is an object or array, the content can be changed.

Arrow functions

The traditional way of defining a function in JavaScript is by using a `function` keyword. The following function gets one argument and just returns the argument value:

```
function hello(greeting) {
    return greeting;
}
```

But when we use the ES6 arrow function, the function looks as follows:

```
const hello = greeting => { greeting }

// function call
hello('Hello World'); // returns Hello World
```

As we can see, by using the arrow function, we have made the declaration of the same function more compact.

When you have more than one argument, you have to wrap the arguments in parentheses and separate the arguments with a comma to use the arrow function effectively. For example, the following function gets two parameters and returns the sum of the parameters:

```
const calcSum = (x, y) => { x + y }

// function call
calcSum(2, 3); // returns 5
```

If the function body is an expression, then you don't need to use the `return` keyword: the expression is always implicitly returned from the function.

However, if the function doesn't have any arguments, then you should use the following syntax:

```
() => { ... }
```

We are going to use lots of arrow functions in our frontend implementation, and so it is important to first understand the basics.

Template literals

Template literals can be used to concatenate strings. The traditional way to concatenate strings is to use the + operator, as follows:

```
var person = {firstName: 'John', lastName: 'Johnson'};
var greeting = "Hello " + ${person.firstName} + " " + ${person.lastName};
```

With the template literals, the syntax is the following. You have to use backticks (` ` `) instead of single or double quotes:

```
var person = {firstName: 'John', lastName: 'Johnson'};
var greeting = `Hello ${person.firstName} ${person.lastName}`;
```

Next, we will learn how to create classes using JavaScript ES6 syntax.

Classes and inheritance

Class definition in ES6 is similar to other object-oriented languages, such as Java or C#. The keyword for defining the classes is `class`. The class can have fields, constructors, and class methods. The following sample code shows the ES6 class:

```
class Person {
    constructor(firstName, lastName) {
        this.firstName = firstName;
        this.lastName = lastName;
    }
}
```

Inheritance is performed with an `extends` keyword. The following sample code shows an `Employee` class that inherits a `Person` class. This means that it inherits all fields from the parent class and can have its own fields that are specific to the `Employee`. In the constructor, we first call the parent class constructor by using the `super` keyword. That call is required by the rest of the code, and you will get an error if it is missing:

```
class Employee extends Person {
    constructor(firstName, lastName, title, salary) {
        super(firstName, lastName);
        this.title= title;
        this.salary = salary;
    }
}
```

Although ES6 is already quite old, it is still only partially supported by modern web browsers. Babel is a JavaScript compiler that is used to compile ES6 to an older version that is compatible with all browsers. You can test the compiler on the Babel website (`https://babeljs.io`). The following screenshot shows the arrow function compiling back to the older JavaScript syntax:

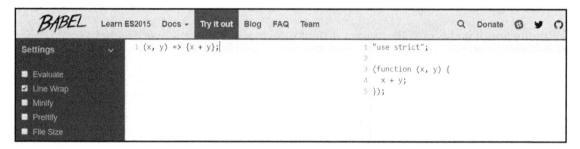

Now that we have learned about the basics of ES6, let's take a look at what JSX and styling is all about.

JSX and styling

JSX is the syntax extension for JavaScript. It is not mandatory to use JSX with React, but there are some benefits that make development easier. JSX, for example, prevents injection attacks because all values are escaped in the JSX before they are rendered. The most useful feature is that you can embed JavaScript expressions in the JSX by wrapping it with curly brackets; this technique will be used a lot in the following chapters. In the following example, we can access the component props when using JSX. The component props are covered in the next section:

```
class Hello extends React.Component {
  render() {
    return <h1>Hello World {this.props.user}</h1>;
  }
}
```

You can also pass a JavaScript expression as props, as shown in the following code:

```
<Hello count={2+2} />
```

JSX is compiled to the `React.createElement()` calls by Babel. You can use both internal or external styling with the React JSX elements. The following are two examples of inline styling. The first one defines the style inside the `div` element, as shown in the following code:

```
<div style={{height: 20, width: 200}}>
  Hello
</div>
```

The second example creates the style object first, which is then used in the `div` element, as shown in the following code. The object name should use the camelCase naming convention:

```
const divStyle = {
  color: 'red',
  height: 30
};

const MyComponent = () => (
  <div style={divStyle}>Hello</div>
);
```

As shown in the previous section, you can import a style sheet to the React component. To reference classes from the external CSS file, you should use a `className` attribute, as shown in the following code:

```
import './App.js';

...

<div className="App-header">
  This is my app
</div>
```

In the next section, we will learn about React props and the state.

Props and the state

Props and the state are the input data for rendering the component. Both props and the state are actually JavaScript objects, and the component is re-rendered when the props or the state change.

The props are immutable, so the component cannot change its props. The props are received from the parent component. The component can access the props through the this.props object. For example, let's take a look at the following component:

```
class Hello extends React.Component {
  render() {
    return <h1>Hello World {this.props.user}</h1>;
  }
}
```

The parent component can send props to the Hello component in the following way:

```
<Hello user="John" />
```

When the Hello component is rendered, it shows the Hello World John text.

The state can be changed inside the component. The initial value of the state is given in the component's constructor. The state can be accessed by using the this.state object. The scope of the state is the component, so it cannot be used outside the component in which it is defined. As you can see in the following example, the props are passed to the constructor as an argument, and the state is initialized in the constructor. The value of the state can then be rendered in JSX using curly brackets, {this.state.user}:

```
class Hello extends React.Component {
  constructor(props) {
    super(props);
    this.state = {user: 'John'}
  }

  render() {
    return <h1>Hello World {this.state.user}</h1>;
  }
}
```

The state can contain multiple values of different types because it is a JavaScript object, as shown in the following example:

```
constructor(props) {
  super(props);
  this.state = {firstName: 'John', lastName: 'Johnson', age: 30}
}
```

The value of the state is changed using the setState method, as shown in the following code:

```
this.setState({firstName: 'Jim', age: 31});  // Change state value
```

You should never update the state by using the = operator because then, React won't re-render the component. The only way to change the state is to use the setState method, which triggers re-rendering, as shown in the following code:

```
this.state.firstName = 'Jim'; // WRONG
```

The setState method is asynchronous, and so you cannot be sure when the state will be updated. The setState method has a callback function that is executed when the state has been updated.

Using the state is always optional, and it increases the complexity of the component. The components that only have the props are called **stateless** components. It will always render the same output when it has the same input, which means they are really easy to test. The components that have both state and props are called **stateful** components. The following is an example of a simple stateless component, and it is defined using a class. You can also define it by using a function:

```
export default class MyTitle extends Component {
  render() {
    return (
     <div>
      <h1>{this.props.text}</h1>
     </div>
    );
 };
};


// The MyTitle component can be then used in other component and text value
is passed to props
<MyTitle text="Hello" />
// Or you can use other component's state
<MyTitle text={this.state.username} />
```

If you are updating the state values that depend on the current state, you should pass an update function to the setState() method instead of the object. A common way of demonstrating this situation is the counter example shown in the following code:

```
// This solution might not work correctly
incrementCounter = () => {
 this.setState({count: this.state.count + 1});
}
```

```
// The correct way is the following
incrementCounter = () => {
  this.setState((prevState) => {
    return {count: prevState.count + 1}
  });
}
```

In the next section, we will learn more about React component life cycle methods

Component life cycle methods

The React component has many life cycle methods that you can override. These methods are executed at certain phases of the component's life cycle. The names of the life cycle methods are logical and you can almost guess when they are going to be executed—the life cycle methods that have a `will` prefix are executed before an action is performed, and the methods with a `did` prefix are executed right after an action is performed.

Mounting is one phase of the component life cycle. It is the moment when the component is created and inserted into the DOM. Two life cycle methods that we have already covered are executed when the component mounts `constructor()` and `render()`.

A useful method in the mounting phase is `componentDidMount()`, which is called after the component has been mounted. This method is suitable for calling some REST APIs to get data, for example. The following sample code gives an example of using the `componentDidMount()` method.

In the following example code, we first set the initial value of `this.state.user` to `John`. Then, when the component is mounted, we change the value to `Jim`:

```
class Hello extends React.Component {
  constructor(props) {
    super(props);
    this.state = {user: 'John'}
  }

  componentDidMount() {
    this.setState({user: 'Jim'});
  }

  render() {
    return <h1>Hello World {this.state.user}</h1>;
  }
}
```

There is also a `componentWillMount()` life cycle method that is called before the component is mounted, but Facebook recommends that you do not use this because it might be used for internal development purposes.

A `shouldComponentUpdate()` method is called when the state or props have been updated and before the component is rendered. The method gets new props as the first argument and a new state as the second argument, and it returns the Boolean value, as shown in the following code. If the returned value is `true`, the component will be re-rendered; otherwise, it won't be re-rendered. This method allows you to avoid useless renders and improves performance:

```
shouldComponentUpdate(nextProps, nextState) {
  // This function should return a boolean, whether the component should
re-render.
  return true;
}
```

A `componentWillUnmount()` life cycle method is called before the component is removed from the DOM. This is a good point at which to clean resources, clear timers, or cancel requests.

Error boundaries are the components that catch JavaScript errors in their child component tree. They should also log these errors and show fallback in the UI. For this, there is a life cycle method called `componentDidCatch()`. It works with the React components in the same way as the standard JavaScript `catch` block.

Stateless components

The React stateless component (a functional component) is just a pure JavaScript function that takes props as an argument and returns a `react` element. The following example shows how a stateless component is used by using the arrow function:

```
import React from 'react';

const HeaderText = (props) => {
 return (
   <h1>
     {props.text}
   </h1>
 )
}

export default HeaderText;
```

Now, when you use functions to define a React component, you don't have to use the `this` keyword. A stateless component defined using a function doesn't have life cycle methods. For example, in the previous `HeaderText` example, you can see that there is no `render()` method.

Our `HeaderText` example component is called a **pure component**. A component is said to be pure if its return value is consistently the same given the same input values. React has introduced `React.memo()`, which optimizes the performance of the pure functional components. In the following code, we wrap our component using `memo()`:

```
import React, { memo } from 'react';

const HeaderText = (props) => {
  return (
    <h1>
      {props.text}
    </h1>
  )
}

export default memo(HeaderText);
```

Now, the component is rendered only if the value of the props is changed. The `React.memo()` phrase also has a second argument, `arePropsEqual()`, which you can use to customize rendering conditions, but we will not cover that here.

The benefits of the functional classes are that you write less code and they are easier to read and understand. Unit testing is also straightforward with pure components.

React hooks

React hooks let you use the state in your components without using a class. You can write your components by using ES6 arrow functions. Let's take a look at how the previous counter example (mentioned in *Props and the state* section) can be performed using React hooks. The hook function that lets you set a state value is called `useState`. It takes one argument, which is the initial value of the state. The following example code creates a state variable called `count`, and the initial value is zero.

The value of the state can now be updated by using the `setCount` function:

```
// count state with initial value 0
const [count, setCount] = useState(0);
```

The counter example now looks like the following when using `setState`. Here, we don't use the `render()` method because we are using a function instead of a component. The function just returns what we want to render:

```
import React, {useState} from 'react';

const Counter = () => {
  const [count, setCount] = useState(0);

  return (
    <div>
      <p>{count}</p>
      <button onClick={() => setCount(count + 1)}>Increment</button>
    </div>
  );
};

export default Counter;
```

If you have multiple states, you can call the `useState` function multiple times, as shown in the following code:

```
const [firstName, setFirstName] = useState('John');
const [lastName, setLastName] = useState('Johnson');
```

Now, you can update states using the `setFirstName` and `setLastName` functions, as shown in the following code:

```
// Update state values
setFirstName('Jim');
setLastName('Palmer');
```

You can also define the state using an object, as follows:

```
const [name, setName] = useState({firstName: 'John', lastName: 'Johnson'});
```

Now, you can update both the `firstName` and `lastName` states using the `setName` function, as follows:

```
setName({firstName: 'Jim', lastName: 'Palmer'})
```

In the following example, we use the object spread syntax (. . .) that was introduced in ES2018. It copies the name of the state object and updates the `firstName` value to be `Jim`:

```
setName({...name, firstName: 'Jim'})
```

When using functions, we don't have class component life cycle methods. Instead, there is a hook called `useEffect` that we can use to get the `componentDidMount`, `componentDidUpdate`, and `componentWillUnmount` mechanisms. When used, the `useEffect` hook runs after every render.

The following code shows the previous counter example, but we have added the `useEffect` hook. Now, when the button is pressed, the `count` state value increases and the UI is re-rendered. After each render, `useEffect` is invoked and we can see the value of `count` in the console:

```
import React, {useState, useEffect} from 'react';

const Counter = () => {
  const [count, setCount] = useState(0);

  // Called after every render
  useEffect(() => {
    console.log('Counter value is now ' + count)
  });

  return (
    <div>
      <p>{count}</p>
      <button onClick={() => setCount(count + 1)}>Increment</button>
    </div>
  );
};

export default Counter;
```

The `useEffect` hook has a second optional argument that you can use to prevent it from running in every render. In the following code, we are stipulating that if the `count` state value is changed (meaning that the previous and current values differ), the `useEffect` function will be invoked. We can also define multiple states in the second argument. If any of these state values are changed, the `useEffect` will be invoked:

```
// Called when count value is changed
useEffect(() => {
  console.log('Counter value is now ' + count);
}, [count]);
```

If you pass an empty array as a second argument, the `useEffect` function runs only after the first render, as shown in the following code:

```
useEffect(() => {
  console.log('Counter value is now ' + count);
}, []);
```

The `useEffect` method can also return a function that will run before every effect, as shown in the following code. With this mechanism, you can clean up each effect from the previous render before running the effect next time:

```
useEffect(() => {
  console.log('Counter value is now ' + count);

  return () => {
      console.log('Clean up function');
  }
}, [count]);
```

Now, if you run a counter app with these changes, you can see what happens in the console, as shown in the following screenshot:

In this section, we learned about React hooks, and we will use them in practice when we start to implement our frontend.

Handling lists with React

For list handling, we introduce a new JavaScript method, `map()`, which is handy when you have to manipulate a list. The `map()` method creates a new array containing the results of calling a function to each element in the original array. In the following example, each array element is multiplied by two:

```
const arr = [1, 2, 3, 4];

const resArr = arr.map(x => x * 2); // resArr = [2, 4, 6, 8]
```

The `map()` method also has the `index` second argument, which is useful when handling lists in React. The list items in React need a unique key that is used to detect rows that have been changed, added, or deleted.

The following example shows components that transform the array of integers to the array of list items and render these in the `ul` element. The component is now defined using the ES6 function:

```
import React from 'react';

const MyList = () => {
  const data = [1, 2, 3, 4, 5];
  const rows = data.map((number, index) =>
    <li key={index}>Listitem {number}</li>
  );

  return (
    <div>
      <ul>{rows}</ul>
    </div>
  );
};

export default MyList;
```

The following screenshot shows what the component looks like when it is rendered:

If the data is an array of objects, it would be nicer to present the data in table format. We do this in roughly the same way as we did with the list, but now we just map the array to table rows and render these in the `table` element, as shown in the following component code:

```
import React from 'react';

const MyList = () => {
  const data = [{brand: 'Ford', model: 'Mustang'},
    {brand:'VW', model: 'Beetle'}, {brand: 'Tesla', model: 'Model S'}];
  const tableRows = data.map((item, index) =>
    <tr key={index}><td>{item.brand}</td><td>{item.model}</td></tr>
    );

  return (
    <div>
      <table><tbody>{tableRows}</tbody></table>
    </div>
  );
};

export default MyList;
```

The following screenshot shows what the component looks like when it is rendered:

Now, you should see the data in the HTML table.

Handling events with React

Event handling in React is similar to handling DOM element events. The difference compared to HTML event handling is that event naming uses camelCase in React. The following sample component code adds an event listener to the button and shows an alert message when the button is pressed:

```
import React from 'react';

const MyComponent = () => {
  // This is called when the button is pressed
  const buttonPressed = () => {
```

```
    alert('Button pressed');
    }
    return (
      <div>
        <button onClick={buttonPressed}>Press Me</button>
      </div>
    );
};

export default MyComponent;
```

In React, you cannot return `false` from the event handler to prevent default behavior. Instead, you should call the `preventDefault()` method. In the following example, we are using a form, and we want to prevent form submission:

```
import React from 'react';

const MyForm = () => {
  // This is called when the form is submitted
  const handleSubmit = (event) => {
    alert('Form submit');
    event.preventDefault(); // Prevents default behavior
  }

  return (
    <form onSubmit={handleSubmit}>
      <input type="submit" value="Submit" />
    </form>
  );
};

export default MyForm;
```

Now, when you press the **Submit** button, you can see the alert and the form will not be submitted.

Handling forms with React

Form handling is a little bit different with React. An HTML form will navigate to the next page when it is submitted. Oftentimes, we will want to invoke a JavaScript function that has access to form data after submission and avoid navigating to the next page. We already covered how to avoid using `submit` in the previous section using `preventDefault()`.

Let's first create a minimalistic form with one input field and the **Submit** button. In order to get the value of the input field, we use the `onChange` event handler. We use the `useState` hook to create a state variable called `text`. When the value of the input field is changed, the new value will be saved to the state.

The `setText(event.target.value)` statement gets the value from the input field and saves it to the state. Finally, we will show the typed value when a user presses the **Submit** button. The following is the source code for our first form:

```
import React, { useState } from 'react';

const MyList = () => {
  const [text, setText] = useState('');

  // Save input box value to state when it has been changed
  const inputChanged = (event) => {
    setText(event.target.value);
  }

  const handleSubmit = (event) => {
    alert(`You typed: ${text}`);
    event.preventDefault();
  }

  return (
    <form onSubmit={handleSubmit}>
      <input type="text" onChange={inputChanged}
          value={text}/>
      <input type="submit" value="Press me"/>
    </form>
  );
};

export default MyList;
```

The following is a screenshot of our form component after the **Submit** button has been pressed:

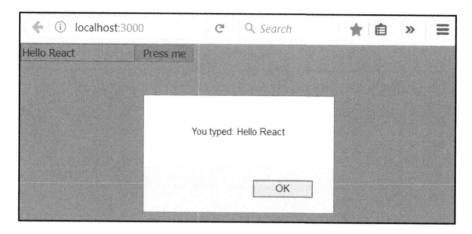

Now is a good time to look at the React developer tools, which are handy tools for debugging React apps. If we open the React developer tools with our React form app and type something into the input field, we can see how the value of the state changes. We can inspect the current value of both the props and the state. The following screenshot shows how the state changes when we type something into the input field:

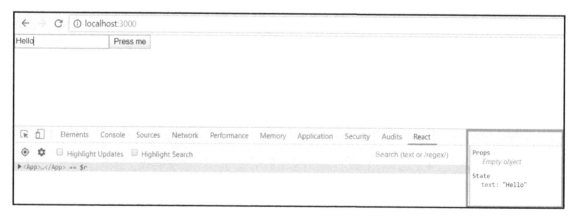

Typically, we have more than one input field in the form. One way to handle multiple input fields is to add as many change handlers as we have input fields, but this creates a lot of boilerplate code, which we want to avoid. Therefore, we add the name attributes to our input fields. We can utilize this in the change handler to identify which input field triggers the change handler. The name attribute value of the input field must be the same as the name of the state in which we want to save the value.

First, we introduce a state called `user` using the `useState` hook, as shown in the following code. The `user` state is an object with three attributes: `firstName`, `lastName`, and `email`:

```
const [user, setUser] = useState({firstName: '', lastName: '', email: ''});
```

The input change handler now looks like the following code. If the input field that triggers the handler is the first name field, then `event.target.name` is `firstName`, and the typed value will be saved to the state object's `firstName` field. Here, we also use the object spread syntax that was introduced in the React hooks section. In this way, we can handle all input fields with the one change handler:

```
const inputChanged = (event) => {
   setUser({...user, [event.target.name]: event.target.value});
}
```

The following is the full source code of the component:

```
import React, { useState } from 'react';

const MyForm = () => {
  const [user, setUser] = useState({firstName: '', lastName: '', email:
''});

  // Save input box value to state when it has been changed
  const inputChanged = (event) => {
    setUser({...user, [event.target.name]: event.target.value});
  }

  const handleSubmit = (event) => {
    alert(`Hello ${user.firstName} ${user.lastName}`);
    event.preventDefault();
  }

  return (
    <form onSubmit={handleSubmit}>
      <label>First name </label>
      <input type="text" name="firstName" onChange={inputChanged}
          value={user.firstName}/><br/>
      <label>Last name </label>
```

```
            <input type="text" name="lastName" onChange={inputChanged}
                value={user.lastName}/><br/>
            <label>Email </label>
            <input type="email" name="email" onChange={inputChanged}
                value={user.email}/><br/>
            <input type="submit" value="Press me"/>
        </form>
    );
};

export default MyForm;
```

The following is a screenshot of our form component after the **Submit** button has been pressed:

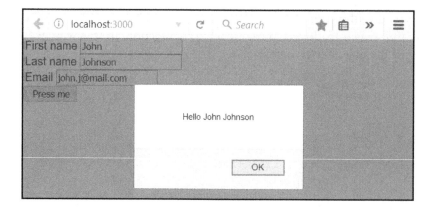

Now, we know how to handle forms with React, and we will use these skills later when we implement our frontend.

Summary

In this chapter, we started to learn about React, which we will be using to build our frontend. Before starting to develop with React, we covered the basics, such as the React component, JSX, props, the state, and hooks. In our frontend development, we use ES6, which makes our code cleaner. We then went through the features that we need for further development. We also learned how to handle forms and events with React.

In the next chapter, we will focus on networking with React. We will also be using the GitHub REST API to learn how to consume a RESTful web service with React.

Questions

1. What is the React component?
2. What are the state and props?
3. How does data flow in the React app?
4. What is the difference between stateless and stateful components?
5. What is JSX?
6. What are component life cycle methods?
7. How should we handle events in React?
8. How should we handle forms in React?

Further reading

Packt has the following great resources for learning about React:

- *Getting Started with React*, by Doel Sengupta, Manu Singhal, Et al: `https://www.packtpub.com/web-development/getting-started-react`
- *React 16 Essentials - Second Edition*, by Adam Boduch and Artemij Fedosejev: `https://www.packtpub.com/web-development/react-16-essentials-second-edition`

Consuming the REST API with React

8

This chapter explains networking with React. We will learn about promises, which make asynchronous code cleaner and more readable. For networking, we will use the `fetch` and `axios` libraries. As an example, we use the GitHub REST API to demonstrate how to consume RESTful web services with React.

In this chapter, we will cover the following topics:

- Using promises
- Using the `fetch` API
- Using the `axios` library
- Practical examples
- How to handle responses from the REST API

Technical requirements

In this book, we are using the Windows operating system, but all tools are available for Linux and macOS as Node.js.

The following GitHub link will also be required: `https://github.com/PacktPublishing/Hands-On-Full-Stack-Development-with-Spring-Boot-2-and-React-Second-Edition/tree/master/Chapter08`.

Using promises

The traditional way to handle an asynchronous operation is to use callback functions for the `success` or `failure` of the operation. One of the callback functions is called, depending on the result of the call. The following example shows the idea of using the callback function:

```
function doAsyncCall(success, failure) {
    // Do some api call
    if (SUCCEED)
        success(resp);
    else
        failure(err);
}

success(response) {
    // Do something with response
}

failure(error) {
    // Handle error
}

doAsyncCall(success, failure);
```

A promise is an object that represents the result of an asynchronous operation. The use of promises simplifies the code when executing asynchronous calls. Promises are non-blocking.

A promise can be in one of three states:

- **Pending**: Initial state
- **Fulfilled**: Successful operation
- **Rejected**: Failed operation

With promises, we can execute asynchronous calls if the API we are using supports promises. In the next example, the asynchronous call is done and, when the response is returned, the function inside `then` is executed and takes the response as an argument:

```
doAsyncCall()
.then(response => // Do something with the response);
```

You can chain many instances of `then` together, which means that you can run multiple asynchronous operations one after another:

```
doAsyncCall()
.then(response => // Get some result from the response)
.then(result => // Do something with the result);
```

You can also add error handling to promises by using `catch()`:

```
doAsyncCall()
.then(response => // Get some result from the response)
.then(result => // Do something with result);
.catch(error => console.error(error))
```

There is a more modern way to handle asynchronous calls, involving `async/await`, which was introduced in ECMAScript 2017. As yet, it is not as widely supported by browsers as promises. `async/await` is actually based on the promises. To use `async/await`, you have to define an `async` function that can contain `await` expressions. The following is an example of an asynchronous call with `async/await`. As you can see, you can write the code in a similar way to synchronous code:

```
doAsyncCall = async () => {
    const response = await fetch('http://someapi.com');
    const result = await response.json();
    // Do something with the result
}
```

For error handling, you can use `try...catch` with `async/await`, as shown in the following example:

```
doAsyncCall = async () => {
  try {
    const response = await fetch('http://someapi.com');
    const result = await response.json();
    // Do something with the result
  }
  catch(err) {
    console.error(err);
  }
}
```

Now, we can start to learn about the `fetch` API, which we can use to make requests in our React apps.

Using the fetch API

With the `fetch` API, you can make web requests. The idea of the `fetch` API is similar to traditional `XMLHttpRequest`, but the `fetch` API also supports promises, which makes it more straightforward to use. You don't have to install any libraries if you are using `fetch`.

The `fetch` API provides a `fetch()` method that has one mandatory argument, which is the path of the resource you are calling. In the case of a web request, it will be the URL of the service. For a simple `GET` method call, which returns a JSON response, the syntax is the following. The `fetch()` method returns a promise that contains the response. You can use the `json()` method to parse the JSON body from the response:

```
fetch('http://someapi.com')
.then(response => response.json())
.then(result => console.log(result));
.catch(error => console.error(error))
```

To use another HTTP method, such as `POST`, you can define it in the second argument of the `fetch` method. The second argument is the object where you can define multiple request settings. The following source code makes the request using the `POST` method:

```
fetch('http://someapi.com', {method: 'POST'})
.then(response => response.json())
.then(result => console.log(result))
.catch(error => console.error(error));
```

You can also add headers inside the second argument. The following `fetch` call contains the `'Content-Type' : 'application/json'` header:

```
fetch('http://someapi.com',
 {
  method: 'POST',
  headers:{'Content-Type': 'application/json'}
 }
.then(response => response.json())
.then(result => console.log(result))
.catch(error => console.error(error));
```

If you have to send JSON-encoded data inside the request body, the syntax is the following:

```
fetch('http://someapi.com',
 {
  method: 'POST',
  headers:{'Content-Type': 'application/json'},
  body: JSON.stringify(data)
 }
```

```
.then(response => response.json())
.then(result => console.log(result))
.catch(error => console.error(error));
```

The `fetch` API is not the only way to execute requests in the React app. There are other libraries that you can use as well, and, in the next topic, we will learn how to use one such popular library called `axios`.

Using the axios library

You can also use other libraries for network calls. One very popular library is `axios` (`https://github.com/axios/axios`), which you can install to your React app with npm:

```
npm install axios
```

You have to execute the following `import axios` command in your React component before using it:

```
import axios from 'axios';
```

The `axios` library has some benefits, such as automatic transformation for JSON data. The following code shows the example call with `axios`:

```
axios.get('http://someapi.com')
.then(response => console.log(response))
.catch(error => console.log(error));
```

The `axios` library has its own call methods for the different HTTP methods. For example, if you want to make a `POST` request and send an object in the body, `axios` provides the `axios.post` method:

```
axios.post('http://someapi.com', {newObject})
.then(response => console.log(response))
.catch(error => console.log(error));
```

Now, we are ready to move on to practical examples involving networking with React.

Practical examples

We will go through two examples of using some open REST APIs. First, we will make a React app that shows the current weather in London. The weather is fetched from **OpenWeatherMap** (`https://openweathermap.org/`). You need to register with **OpenWeatherMap** to get an API key. We will use a free account as that is sufficient for our needs. When you have registered, navigate to your account info to find the **API keys** tab. There, you'll see the API key that you need for your React `weatherapp`:

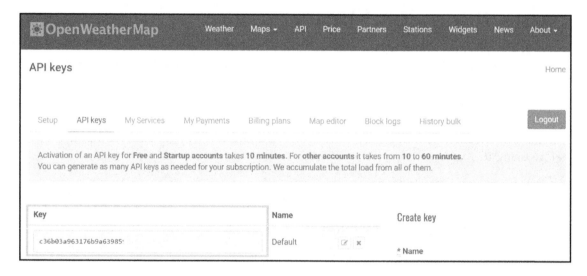

Let's create a new React app with `create-react-app`. Open PowerShell, or another terminal you are using, and type the following command:

    npx create-react-app weatherapp

Move to the `weatherapp` folder:

    cd weatherapp

Start your app with the following command:

    npm start

Open your project folder with VS Code and open the `App.js` file in the editor view. Remove all code inside the `<div className="App"></div>` divider. Now, your source code should look like the following:

```
import React from 'react';
import './App.css';

function App() {
  return (
    <div className="App">
    </div>
  );
}

export default App;
```

Next, create a new component called `WeatherApp` in the `src` folder. We will use now class-based component for fetching but you can also use functional component and use `useEffect` hook for fetching. The following is the starter code of the `WeatherApp` component.

```
import React, { Component } from 'react';
import './App.css';

class WeatherApp extends Component {
  render() {
    return (
      <div className="App">
      </div>
    );
  }
}

export default WeatherApp;
```

First, we add a necessary constructor and state in the `WeatherApp` component. We will show the temperature, description, and weather icon in our app. Therefore, we have to define three state values. We will also add one boolean state to indicate the status of `fetch` loading. The following is the source code of the constructor:

```
constructor(props) {
  super(props);
  this.state = {temp: 0, desc: '', icon: '', loading: true}
}
```

If you have installed *Reactjs code snippets* to VS Code, you can create a default constructor automatically by typing `con`. There are lots of different shortcuts for typical React methods, such as `cdm` for `componentDidMount()`.

When you are using a REST API, you should first inspect the response to be able to get values from the JSON data. In the following example, you can see the address that returns the current weather for London. Copy the address to a browser and you can see the JSON response data:

```
api.openweathermap.org/data/2.5/weather?q=London&units=Metric&APIkey=YOUR_K
EY
```

From the response, you can see that `temp` can be accessed using `main.temp`. Then, you can see that `description` and `icon` are inside the `weather` array, which has only one element, and we can access it using `weather[0].description` and `weather[0].icon`:

```
api.openweathermap.org/data/2.5/weather?q=
{ ▼ 13 properties, 442 bytes
  "coord": { ▼ 2 properties, 37 bytes
    "lon": -0.13,
    "lat": 51.51
  },
  "weather": [ ▼ 1 item, 73 bytes
    { ▼ 4 properties, 71 bytes
      "id": 804,
      "main": "Clouds",
      "description": "overcast clouds",
      "icon": "04d"
    }
  ],
  "base": "stations",
  "main": { ▼ 5 properties, 72 bytes
    "temp": 15.45,
    "pressure": 1014,
    "humidity": 45,
    "temp_min": 14,
    "temp_max": 17
  },
```

The REST API call is executed using `fetch` in the `componentDidMount()` life cycle method. After the successful response, we save the weather data to the state and change the `loading` state to `false`. After the state has been changed, the component will be re-rendered. We will implement the `render()` method in the next step. The following is the source code of the `componentDidMount()` method:

```
componentDidMount() {
  fetch('http://api.openweathermap.org/data/2.5/weather?
    q=London&units=Metric
    &APIkey=YOUR_KEY')
  .then(response => response.json())
  .then(responseData => {
    this.setState({
        temp: responseData.main.temp,
        desc: responseData.weather[0].description,
        icon: responseData.weather[0].icon,
        loading: false
      })
  })
    .catch(err => console.error(err));
}
```

After you have added the `componentDidMount()` method, the request is executed when the component is mounted. We can check that everything is done correctly using the React developer tool. Open your app in a browser and open your browser developer tool's **React** tab. Now, you can see that the state is updated with the values from the response:

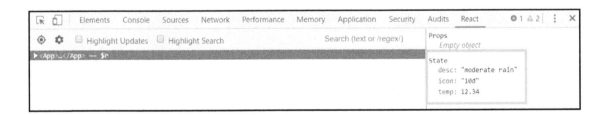

You can also check from the **Network** tab that the request status is **200 OK**. Finally, we implement the `render()` method to show the weather values. We are using conditional rendering; otherwise, we get an error because we don't have image code in the first render call and the image upload won't succeed. To show the weather icon, we have to add `http://openweathermap.org/img/w/` before the icon code, and `.png` after the icon code. Then, we can set the concatenated image URL to the `img` element's `src` attribute. `Temperature` and `Description` are shown in the paragraph element. The °C HTML entity shows the degree Celsius symbol:

```
render() {
  const imgSrc =
`http://openweathermap.org/img/w/${this.state.icon}.png`;

  if (this.state.loading) {
   return <p>Loading</p>;
  }
  else {
   return (
      <div className="App">
        <p>Temperature: {this.state.temp} °C</p>
        <p>Description: {this.state.desc}</p>
        <img src={imgSrc} alt="Weather icon" />
      </div>
   );
  }
}
```

Finally, import `WeatherApp` to `App.js` file and render it:

```
import React from 'react';
import './App.css';
import WeatherApp from './WeatherApp';

function App() {
  return (
    <div className="App">
      <WeatherApp />
    </div>
  );
}

export default App;
```

Now, your app should be ready. When you open it in a browser, it should look like the following screenshot:

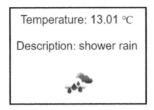

The source code for the entire `WeatherApp.js` file appears as follows:

```
import React, { Component } from 'react';
import './App.css';

class WeatherApp extends Component {
  constructor(props) {
    super(props);
    this.state = {temp: 0, desc: '', icon: '', loading: true}
  }

  componentDidMount() {
    fetch('http://api.openweathermap.org/data/2.5/weather?
      q=London&units=Metric&APIkey=YOUR_KEY')
    .then(response => response.json())
    .then(responseData => {
      this.setState({
          temp: responseData.main.temp,
         desc: responseData.weather[0].description,
         icon: responseData.weather[0].icon,
         loading: false
        });
    });
  }
  render() {
    const imgSrc = 'http://openweathermap.org/img/w/' +
    this.state.icon + '.png';

    if (this.state.loading) {
      return <p>Loading</p>;
    }
    else {
      return (
        <div className="App">
          <p>Temperature: {this.state.temp} °C</p>
          <p>Description: {this.state.desc}</p>
```

```
            <img src={imgSrc} alt="Weather icon" />
         </div>
       );
     }
   }
 }

export default WeatherApp;
```

In this second example, we are going to use the GitHub API to fetch repositories according to a keyword. Following the same steps as in the previous example, create a new React app called `restgithub`. Start the app and open the project folder with VS Code.

Remove the extra code inside the `<div className="App"></div>` divider from the `App.js` file and, again, your `App.js` code should look like the following sample code:

```
import React from 'react';
import './App.css';

function App() {
  return (
    <div className="App">
    </div>
  );
}

export default App;
```

The URL of the GitHub REST API is the following:

```
https://api.github.com/search/repositories?q=KEYWORD
```

Let's inspect the JSON response by typing the URL into a browser and using the `react` keyword. From the response, we can see that repositories are returned as a JSON array called `items`. From the individual repositories, we will show the `full_name` and `html_url` values.

We will present the data in the table and use the `map` function to transform the values to table rows, as shown in the previous chapter:

We are going to make the REST API call with the `keyword` from the user input. Therefore, we can't make the REST API call after the first render because, in that phase, we don't have the user input available. One way to implement this is to create an input field and button. The user types the keyword into the input field and the REST API call is done when the button is pressed. We need two states, one for the user input, and one for the data from the JSON response. Now, we are using functional component. The following is the source code that introduce two states called `data` and `keyword` using `useState` hook. The type of `data` state is an array because repositories are returned as JSON arrays in the response:

```
const [data, setData] = useState([]);
const [keyword, setKeyword] = useState('');
```

Next, we implement the input field and the button in the `return` statement. We also have to add a change listener to our input field to be able to save the input value to `state`, called `keyword`. The button has a click listener that invokes the function that will do the REST API call with the given `keyword`. Note, we don't have to use `this` keyword in the functional component:

```
const fetchData = () => {
  // REST API call comes here
}
const handleChange = (e) => {
  setKeyword(e.target.value);
}

return (
  <div className="App">
    <input type="text" onChange={handleChange} />
    <button onClick={fetchData} value={keyword} >fetch</button>
  </div>
);
```

In the `fetchData` function, we concatenate the `url` and `keyword` state by using template literals. Then, we save the `items` array from the response to the state, called `data`. The following is the source code of the `fetchData` function:

```
const fetchData = () => {
  const url = `https://api.github.com/search/repositories?q=${keyword}`;
  fetch(url)
  .then(response => response.json())
  .then(responseData => {
    setData(responseData.items);
  });
}
```

We first use the `map` function to transform the `data` state to table rows. The `url` repository will be the `href` value of the link element. The html `table` is also added to the `return` statement:

```
const tableRows = data.map((item, index) =>
  <tr key={index}><td>{item.full_name}</td>
  <td><a href={item.html_url}>{item.html_url}</a></td></tr>);

return (
  <div className="App">
    <input type="text" onChange={handleChange} />
    <button onClick={fetchData} value={keyword} >fetch</button>
    <table><tbody>{tableRows}</tbody></table>
```

```
  </div>
);
```

The following screenshot shows the final app when using the `React` keyword in the REST API call:

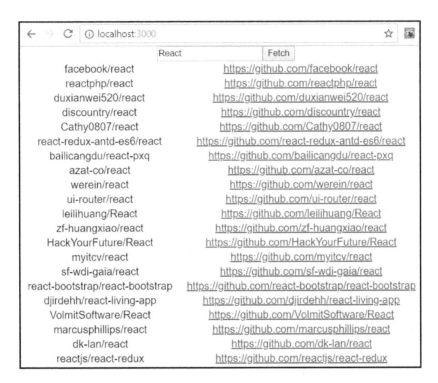

The source code of the whole `App.js` file looks like the following:

```
import React, { useState } from 'react';
import './App.css';

function App() {
  const [data, setData] = useState([]);
  const [keyword, setKeyword] = useState('');

  const fetchData = () => {
    const url = `https://api.github.com/search/repositories?q=${keyword}`;
    fetch(url)
    .then(response => response.json())
    .then(responseData => {
      setData(responseData.items);
```

```
    });
  }

  const handleChange = (e) => {
    setKeyword(e.target.value);
  }

  const tableRows = data.map((item, index) =>
    <tr key={index}><td>{item.full_name}</td>
    <td><a href={item.html_url}>{item.html_url}</a></td></tr>);

  return (
    <div className="App">
      <input type="text" onChange={handleChange} />
      <button onClick={fetchData} value={keyword} >fetch</button>
      <table><tbody>{tableRows}</tbody></table>
    </div>
  );
}

export default App;
```

Now, we have learned about networking with React and we will utilize these skills in the frontend implementation.

Summary

In this chapter, we focused on networking with React. We started with promises, which make asynchronous network calls easier to implement. This a cleaner way to handle calls, and much better than using traditional callback functions.

In this book, we are using the `fetch` API for networking. Therefore, we went through the basics of using `fetch`. We implemented two practical React apps using the `fetch` API to call REST APIs and we presented the response data in the browser.

In the next chapter, we will look at some useful React components that we are going to use in our frontend.

Questions

1. What is a promise?
2. What is `fetch`?
3. How should you call the REST API from the React app?
4. How should you handle the response of the REST API call?

Further reading

Packt has other great resources available for learning about React. These are as follows:

- *Getting Started with React*, by Doel Sengupta, Manu Singhal, et al (`https://www.packtpub.com/web-development/getting-started-react`)
- *React 16 Essentials – Second Edition*, by Adam Boduch, and Artemij Fedosejev (`https://www.packtpub.com/web-development/react-16-essentials-second-edition`)

Useful Third-Party Components for React

9

React is component-based, and we can find a lot of useful third-party components that we can use in our apps. In this chapter, we are going to look at several components that we are going to use in our frontend. We will examine how to find suitable components and how you can then use these in your own apps.

In this chapter, we will cover the following topics:

- How to find third-party React components
- How to install components
- How to use the React Table component
- How to use the Material-UI component library
- How to manage routing in React

Technical requirements

In this book, we will be using the Windows operating system, but all the tools are available for Linux and macOS as well.

Node.js also has to be installed, and the following GitHub link will be required: `https://github.com/PacktPublishing/Hands-On-Full-Stack-Development-with-Spring-Boot-2-and-React-Second-Edition/tree/master/Chapter09`.

Using third-party React components

There are lots of nice React components available for different purposes. Our first task is to find a suitable component for your needs. One good site for searching components is **JS.coach** (`https://js.coach/`). You just have to type in a keyword, search, and select **React** from the list of frameworks. In the following screenshot, you can see a search of the `table` components for **React**:

Another good source for React components is `awesome-react-components` (`https://github.com/brillout/awesome-react-components`).

Components often have good documentation that helps you to utilize them in your own React app. Let's see how we can install a third-party component to our app and start to use it. Navigate to the **JS.coach** site, type `list` to search the input field, and filter by **React**. From the search results, you can find the list component, called **react-tiny-virtual-list**:

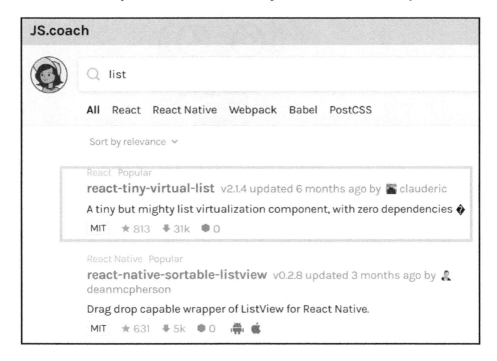

Click the component link to see more detailed information pertaining to the component. Quite often, you can find the installation instructions there and some simple examples of how to use the component. The info page often provides the address of a component's website or GitHub repository, where you can find the full documentation:

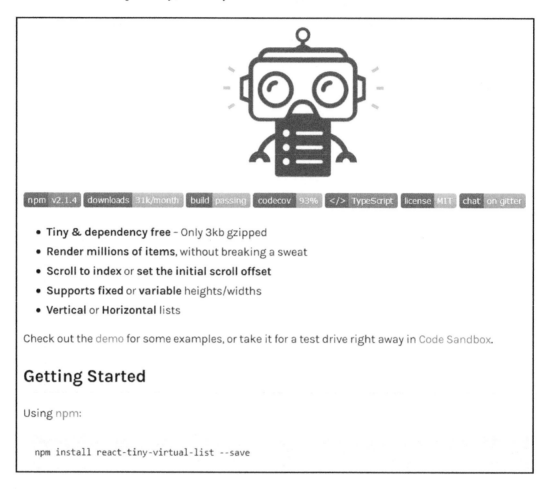

As you can see from the component's info page, components are installed using npm. The syntax of the command is as follows:

```
npm install component_name
```

Or, if you are using yarn, it is as follows:

```
yarn add component_name
```

The npm install and yarn add commands save the component's dependency to the package.json file that is in the root folder of your React app.

Now, we install the react-tiny-virtual-list component to the myapp React app that we created in Chapter 6, *Setting Up the Environment and Tools - Frontend*. You then have to move to your app root folder and type the following command:

```
npm install react-tiny-virtual-list
```

If you open the package.json file from your app root folder, you can see that the component is now added to the dependencies:

```json
{
  "name": "myapp",
  "version": "0.1.0",
  "private": true,
  "dependencies": {
    "react": "^16.8.6",
    "react-dom": "^16.8.6",
    "react-scripts": "3.0.1",
    "react-tiny-virtual-list": "^2.2.0"
  },
  "scripts": {
    "start": "react-scripts start",
    "build": "react-scripts build",
    "test": "react-scripts test",
    "eject": "react-scripts eject"
  },
  "eslintConfig": {
    "extends": "react-app"
  },
  "browserslist": {
    "production": [
      ">0.2%",
      "not dead",
      "not op_mini all"
    ],
    "development": [
      "last 1 chrome version",
      "last 1 firefox version",
      "last 1 safari version"
    ]
  }
}
```

Installed components are saved to the node_modules folder in your app. If you open that folder, you should find the react-tiny-virtual-list folder:

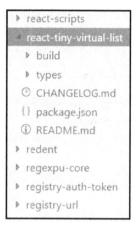

Now, if you push your React app source code to GitHub, you should not include node_modules because that folder is large. create-react-app contains the .gitignore file, which excludes the node_modules folder from the repository. The content of the .gitignore file appears as follows:

```
# See https://help.github.com/ignore-files/ for more about ignoring files.

# dependencies
/node_modules

# testing
/coverage

# production
/build

# misc
.DS_Store
.env.local
.env.development.local
.env.test.local
.env.production.local

npm-debug.log*
yarn-debug.log*
yarn-error.log*
```

The idea is that when you clone your app from the GitHub, you type the `npm install` command, which reads dependencies from the `package.json` file and downloads these to your app.

The final step to start using your installed component is to import it into the files where you are using it:

```
import VirtualList from 'react-tiny-virtual-list';
```

You have now learned how to install and start to use React components.

React Table

React Table (`https://react-table.js.org`) is a flexible table component for React apps. It has many useful features, such as filtering, sorting, and pivoting. Let's use the GitHub REST API app that we created in Chapter 8, *Consuming the REST API with React*:

1. To install the `react-table` component, open PowerShell and move to the `restgithub` folder, which is the root folder of the app. Install the component by typing the following command:

   npm install react-table

2. Open the `App.js` file with VS Code and remove `tablerows` and the `table` inside the `return`. Now, the `App.js` file should appear as follows:

   ```
   import React, { useState } from 'react';
   import './App.css';

   function App() {
     const [data, setData] = useState([]);
     const [keyword, setKeyword] = useState('');

     const fetchData = () => {
       const url =
   `https://api.github.com/search/repositories?q=${keyword}`;
       fetch(url)
       .then(response => response.json())
       .then(responseData => {
         setData(responseData.items);
       });
     }
     const handleChange = (e) => {
       setKeyword(e.target.value);
   ```

```
    }

    return (
      <div className="App">
        <input type="text" onChange={handleChange} />
        <button onClick={fetchData} value={keyword}
>fetch</button>
        </div>
      );
    }

    export default App;
```

3. Import the `react-table` component and style sheet by adding the following lines at the beginning of the `App.js` file:

```
import ReactTable from "react-table";
import 'react-table/react-table.css';
```

4. To fill the React Table with data, you have to pass the `data` prop to the component. Data can be an array or object and therefore we can use our state, called `data`. Columns are defined using the `columns` prop, and this prop is required:

```
<ReactTable
  data={data}
  columns={columns}
/>
```

5. We will define our `columns` by creating an array of column objects. In a column object, you have to define at least the header of the column and the data accessor. The data accessor values come from our REST API response data. You can see that our response data contains an object called `owner`, and we can show these values using the `owner.field_name` syntax:

```
const columns = [{
    Header: 'Name',  // Header of the column
    accessor: 'full_name' // Value accessor
  }, {
    Header: 'URL',
    accessor: 'html_url',
  }, {
    Header: 'Owner',
    accessor: 'owner.login',
}]
```

6. Add the React Table component to our `return` statement, and then the source code looks like the following:

```
const columns = [{
   Header: 'Name', // Header of the column
   accessor: 'full_name' // Value accessor
 }, {
   Header: 'URL',
   accessor: 'html_url',
 }, {
   Header: 'Owner',
   accessor: 'owner.login',
 }]

return (
   <div className="App">
     <input type="text" onChange={handleChange} />
     <button onClick={fetchData} value={keyword} >fetch</button>
     <ReactTable data={data} columns={columns} />
   </div>
);
```

7. Run the app and navigate to `localhost:3000`. The table looks quite nice. It has sorting and paging available by default, as demonstrated in the following screenshot:

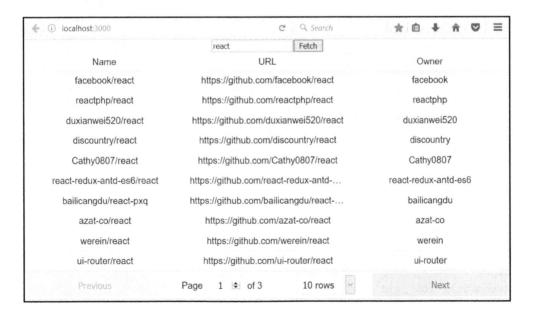

Filtering is disabled by default, but you can enable it using the `filterable` prop in the `ReactTable` component. You can also set the page size of the table:

```
<ReactTable
    data={this.state.data}
    columns={columns}
    filterable={true}
    defaultPageSize = {10}
/>
```

Now, you should see the filter element in your table. You can filter using any column, but there is also an option to set the filtering and sorting at the column level:

You can find different props for the table and columns from the React Table website.

Cell renderers can be used to customize the content of the table cell. The following example shows how you can render a button to a table cell. The function in the cell renderer passes `value` as the argument and, in this case, the value will be `full_name`, which is defined in the accessor of the column. The other option is to pass a row, which passes the whole `row` object to the function. Then, you have to define the `btnClick` function, which is invoked when the button is pressed and you can do something with the value that is sent to the function:

```
const btnClick = (value) => {
  alert(value);
}

const columns = [{
  Header: 'Name', // Header of the column
  accessor: 'full_name' // Value accessor
}, {
  Header: 'URL',
  accessor: 'html_url',
}, {
  Header: 'Owner',
```

```
  accessor: 'owner.login',
}, {
id: 'button',
sortable: false,
filterable: false,
width: 100,
accessor: 'full_name',
Cell: ({value}) => (<button onClick={() => {btnClick(value)}}>Press
me</button>)
}]
```

The following is the screenshot of the table with buttons:

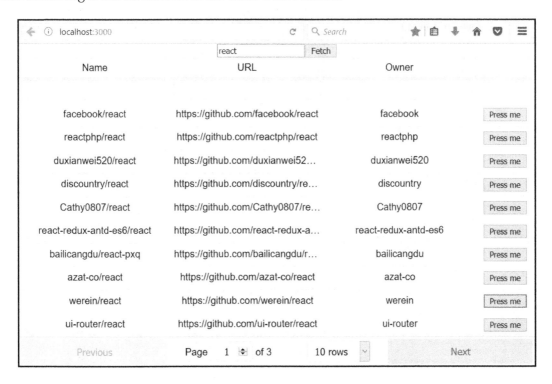

Next, we will start to use the Material-UI component library, which is one of the most popular React component libraries.

Material-UI component library

Material-UI is the React component library that implements Google's material design. It contains a lot of different components, such as buttons, lists, tables, and cards, that you can use to achieve a nice and uniform UI. We will create a small shopping list app and style the user interface using Material-UI components:

1. Create a new React app called `shoppinglist`:

   ```
   npx create-react-app shoppinglist
   ```

2. Open the shopping list app with VS Code. Install Material-UI by typing the following command in the project root folder to PowerShell or any suitable terminal you are using:

   ```
   npm install @material-ui/core
   ```

   OR with yarn

   ```
   yarn add @material-ui/core
   ```

3. Open the `App.js` file and remove all the code inside the `App` div. Now, your `App.js` file should look like the following and you should see an empty page in the browser:

   ```
   import React from 'react';
   import './App.css';

   function App() {
     return (
       <div className="App">
       </div>
     );
   }

   export default App;
   ```

4. We will use the Material-UI `AppBar` component to show the toolbar in our app. Import the `AppBar`, `ToolBar`, and `Typography` components to your `App.js` file:

   ```
   import AppBar from '@material-ui/core/AppBar';
   import Toolbar from '@material-ui/core/Toolbar';
   import Typography from '@material-ui/core/Typography';
   ```

5. Add the following code to your `App.js` `return` statement.
The `Typography` component provides predefined type sizes and we will use this in our toolbar text:

```
return (
  <div className="App">
    <AppBar position="static" color="default">
      <Toolbar>
        <Typography variant="h6" color="inherit">
          SHOPPINGLIST
        </Typography>
      </Toolbar>
    </AppBar>
  </div>
);
```

Now, your app should appear as follows:

6. In the `App.js` component, we only require one state to keep the shopping list items. One shopping list item contains two fields—`product` and `amount`. We also need a method to add new items to the list. The following is the source code of the state using `useState` hook and the method for adding new items to the list. In the `addItem` method, we are using a spread notation (`...`), that is used to add a new item at the beginning of the existing array:

```
const [items, setItems] = React.useState([]);

const addItem = (item) => {
  setItems([item, ...items]);
}
```

7. Add a new component for adding shopping items. Create a new file called `AddItem.js` to the root folder of the app. Let's use React Hooks in the new component. Therefore, we use the arrow function to define our component. Add the following code to your `AddItem.js` file:

```
import React from 'react';

const AddItem = (props) => {
```

```
      return (
        <div>
        </div>
      );
    }

    export default AddItem;
```

The `AddItem` component will use the Material-UI modal dialog for collecting the data. In the form, we will add two input fields (`product` and `amount`) and a button that calls the `addItem` function. To be able to call the `addItem` function, which is in the `App.js` component, we have to pass it in a prop when rendering the `AddItem` component. Outside the modal `Dialog` component, we will add a button that opens the modal form when it is pressed. This button is the only visible element when the component is rendered initially.

The `Dialog` component has one prop called `open` and, if the value is `true`, the dialog is visible. The default value of that prop will be `false` and the dialog is hidden. The button that opens the modal dialog sets the `open` state value to `true` and the dialog opens. We also have to handle the change event of the input fields, so that we can access the values that have been typed. When the button inside the modal form is clicked, the `addItem` function is called and the modal form is closed by setting `open` value to `false`. The function creates an object from the input field values and calls the `App.js` component's `addItem` function, which finally adds a new item to the state array and re-renders the UI. The following steps describe the implementation of the modal form:

1. We have to import the following Material-UI components for the modal form: `Dialog`, `DialogActions`, `DialogContent`, and `DialogTitle`. And, as regards the UI of the modal form, we require the following components: `Button` and `TextField`. Add the following imports to your `AddItem.js` file:

   ```
   import Button from '@material-ui/core/Button';
   import TextField from '@material-ui/core/TextField';
   import Dialog from '@material-ui/core/Dialog';
   import DialogActions from '@material-ui/core/DialogActions';
   import DialogContent from '@material-ui/core/DialogContent';
   import DialogTitle from '@material-ui/core/DialogTitle';
   ```

2. Next, we will introduce one state called `open` by using React Hooks and two functions for opening and closing the modal dialog. The default value of the `open` state is `false`. The `handleOpen` function sets the `open` state to `true`, and the `handleClose` function sets it to `false`:

   ```
   const AddItem = (props) => {
   ```

```
const [open, setOpen] = React.useState(false);

const handleOpen = () => {
  setOpen(true);
}

const handleClose = () => {
  setOpen(false);
}

return (
  <div>
  </div>
);
}
```

3. We will add `Dialog` and `Button` components inside the `return` statement. We have one button outside the dialog that will be visible when the component is rendered for the first time. When the button is pressed, it calls the `handleOpen` function, which opens the dialog. Inside the dialog, we have two buttons—one for canceling and one for adding a new item. The add button calls the `addItem` function, which we will implement later.

```
return (
  <div>
    <Button style={{marginTop: 10}} variant="outlined"
color="primary" onClick={handleOpen}>
      Add Item
    </Button>
    <Dialog open={open} onClose={handleClose} aria-
labelledby="form-dialog-title">
      <DialogTitle id="form-dialog-title">New Item</DialogTitle>
      <DialogContent>
      </DialogContent>
      <DialogActions>
        <Button onClick={handleClose} color="primary">
          Cancel
        </Button>
        <Button onClick={addItem} color="primary">
          Add
        </Button>
      </DialogActions>
    </Dialog>
  </div>
);
```

4. To collect data from a user, we have to introduce one more state. The state is an object with two attributes—`product` and `amount`. Add the following line after the line where you introduced the open state:

```
const [item, setItem] = React.useState({product: '', amount: ''});
```

5. Inside the `DialogContent` component, we will add two inputs to collect data from a user. There, we use the `TextField` Material-UI component that we have already imported. The value attributes of text fields must be the same as the state where we want to save the typed value. In the product field, it is `item.product`, and, in the amount field, it is `item.amount`:

```
<DialogContent>
  <TextField autoFocus margin="dense" value={item.product}
    onChange={handleChange} name="product" label="Product"
fullWidth />
  <TextField autoFocus margin="dense" value={item.amount}
    onChange={handleChange} name="amount" label="Amount" fullWidth
/>
</DialogContent>
```

6. Next, we have to implement the `handleChange` function, which is invoked when we type something to the input fields. As we have already learned in Chapter 7, *Getting Started with React*, the following function saves values from the input field to the `item` state:

```
// Handle the change of input field values
const handleChange = (e) => {
  setItem({...item, [e.target.name]:e.target.value})
}
```

7. Finally, we have to add a function that calls the `addItem` function that we get in the `props` and pass a new `item` into that function. The new item is now the `item` state that contains the shopping item that the user typed in. Because we get the `addItem` function from the props, we can call it using the `props` keyword. Then, we will also call the `handleClose` function, which closes the modal dialog:

```
// Calls addItem function (in props) and pass item state into it.
const addItem = () => {
  props.addItem(item);
  handleClose();
}
```

8. Now, our `AddItem` component is ready and we have to import it to our `App.js` file and render it there. Add the following import to your `App.js` file:

```
import AddItem from './AddItem';
```

9. Add the `AddItem` component to the `return` statement in the `App.js` file. Pass the `addItem` function in a prop to the `AddItem` component:

```
// App.js return
return (
  <div className="App">
    <AppBar position="static" color="default">
      <Toolbar>
        <Typography variant="h6" color="inherit">
          SHOPPINGLIST
        </Typography>
      </Toolbar>
    </AppBar>
    <AddItem addItem={addItem} />
  </div>
);
```

Now, if you open your app in the browser and press the **Add Item** button, you will see the modal form opening and you can type a new item. The modal form is closed when you press the **ADD** button:

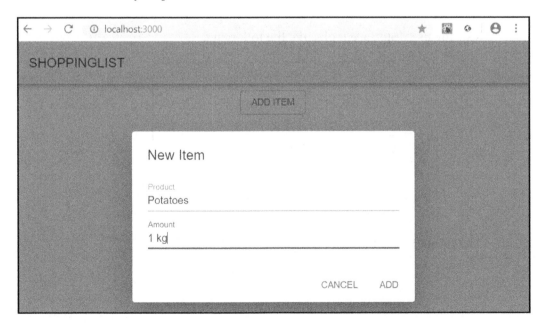

10. Next, we will add a list to the main page that shows our shopping items. For that, we will use the Material-UI `List` and `ListItem` components. Import the components and use `ListItem` in the map function where `listItems` are created and render the `List` component. We will show the amount of product in the secondary text of the `ListItemText` component:

```
// App.js
// Import List, ListItem and ListItemText components
import List from '@material-ui/core/List';
import ListItem from '@material-ui/core/ListItem';
import ListItemText from '@material-ui/core/ListItemText';

// Use List and ListItem in return
return (
 <div className="App">
   <AppBar position="static" color="default">
   <Toolbar>
     <Typography variant="h6" color="inherit">
       SHOPPINGLIST
     </Typography>
    </Toolbar>
   </AppBar>
   <AddItem addItem={addItem} />
   <List>{listItems}</List>
 </div>
);
```

Now, the user interface looks like the following:

Next, we will learn how to use React Router, a popular routing library.

Routing

There are multiple solutions available for routing in React. The most popular one, which we are using, is React Router (`https://github.com/ReactTraining/react-router`). For web applications, React Router provides a package called `react-router-dom`.

To start using React Router, we have to install it with the following command:

```
npm install react-router-dom
```

There are four different components in `react-router-dom` that are required to implement routing. `BrowserRouter` is the router for web-based applications. The `Route` component renders the defined component if the given locations match. The following are two examples of the `Route` component. The first one renders the `Contact` component when the user navigates to the `/contact` end path. You can also use inline rendering with the `Route` component, as shown in the following example:

```
<Route path="/contact" component={Contact} />
// Route with inline rendering
<Route path="/links" render={() => <h1>Links</h1>} />
```

The `Switch` component wraps multiple `Route` components. The `Link` component provides navigation to your application. The following example shows the `Contact` link and navigates to the `/contact` endpoint when the link is clicked:

```
<Link to="/contact">Contact</Link>
```

The following example shows how to use these components in practice. Let's create a new React app, called `routerapp`, using `create-react-app`. Open the app folder with VS Code and open the `App.js` file to editor view. Import components from the `react-router-dom` package and remove extra code from the `return` statement. Following these modifications, your `App.js` source code should appear as follows:

```
import React from 'react';
import './App.css';
import { BrowserRouter, Switch, Route, Link } from 'react-router-dom'

function App() {
  return (
    <div className="App">
    </div>
  );
}

export default App;
```

Let's first create two simple components that we can use in routing. Create two new files, called `Home.js` and `Contact.js`, in the application root folder. Then, add headers to the `return` statements to show the name of the component. The code of the component is as follows:

```
// Contact.js
import React from 'react';

const Contact = () => {
  return (
    <div>
      <h1>Contact.js</h1>
    </div>
  );
}

export default Contact;

// Home.js
import React from 'react';

const Home = () => {
  return (
    <div>
      <h1>Home.js</h1>
    </div>
  );
}

export default Home;
```

Open the `App.js` file, and then add a router that allows us to navigate between the components:

```
import React from 'react';
import './App.css';
import { BrowserRouter, Switch, Route, Link } from 'react-router-dom'
import Contact from './Contact';
import Home from './Home';

function App() {
  return (
    <div className="App">
      <BrowserRouter>
        <div>
          <Link to="/">Home</Link>{' '}
          <Link to="/contact">Contact</Link>{' '}
```

```
        <Link to="/links">Links</Link>{' '}
        <Switch>
          <Route exact path="/" component={Home} />
          <Route path="/contact" component={Contact} />
          <Route path="/links" render={() => <h1>Links</h1>} />
          <Route render={() => <h1>Page not found</h1>} />
        </Switch>
      </div>
    </BrowserRouter>
  </div>
  );
}

export default App;
```

Now, when you start the app, you will see the links and the Home component, which is shown in the root end path (localhost:3000/) as defined in the first Route component. The exact keyword in the first Route component means that the path must match exactly. If you remove that, then the routing always goes to the Home component:

When you press the **Contact** link, the Contact component is rendered:

At this point, you have learned how to install and use third-party components with React. These skills will be required in the following chapters when we start to build our frontend.

Summary

In this chapter, we learned how to use third-party React components. We familiarized ourselves with several components that we are going to use in our frontend. React Table is the table component with built-in features, such as sorting, paging, and filtering. React Skylight is the modal form component that we will use in our frontend to create forms for adding and editing items.

Material-UI is the component library that provides multiple user interface components that implement Google's material design. We also learned how to use React Router for routing in React applications.

In the next chapter, we will build an environment for frontend development.

Questions

1. How should you find components for React?
2. How should you install components?
3. How should you use the React Table component?
4. How should you use the Material-UI component library?
5. How should you implement routing in a React application?

Further reading

Packt has other great resources available for learning about React. These are as follows:

- *Getting Started with React*, by Doel Sengupta, Manu Singhal, et al (`https://www.packtpub.com/web-development/getting-started-react`)
- *React 16 Essentials – Second Edition*, by Adam Boduch, and Artemij Fedosejev (`https://www.packtpub.com/web-development/react-16-essentials-second-edition`)

Section 3: Full Stack Development

In this section, we will combine the Spring Boot backend and the React frontend. We will use the Spring Boot backend that we created in Section 1, *Backend Programming with Spring Boot,* to create a frontend with React. The frontend provides us with all of the CRUD operations.

This section covers the following chapters:

Setting Up the Frontend for Our Spring Boot RESTful Web Service

10

This chapter explains the steps that are required to start the development of the frontend part. We will first define the functionalities that we are developing. Then, we will do a mock-up of the UI. As a backend, we will use our Spring Boot application from Chapter 5, *Securing and Testing Your Backend*. We will begin development using the unsecured version of the backend. Finally, we will create the React app, which we will use in our frontend development.

In this chapter, we will cover the following topics:

- Why a mock-up is necessary and how to go about it
- Preparing our Spring Boot backend for frontend development
- Creating the React app for the frontend

Technical requirements

The Spring Boot application that we created in Chapter 5, *Securing and Testing Your Backend*, is required.

Node.js also has to be installed, and the code samples available at the following GitHub link will be required to follow along with the examples in this chapter: https://github.com/PacktPublishing/Hands-On-Full-Stack-Development-with-Spring-Boot-2.0-and-React-Second-Edition/tree/master/Chapter10.

Mocking up the UI

In the first few chapters of this book, we created a car database backend that provides the RESTful API. Now, it is time to start building the frontend to our application. We will create a frontend that lists cars from the database and provides paging, sorting, and filtering. There is a button that opens the modal form to add new cars to the database. In each row of the car table, there is a button to delete the car from the database. Table rows are also editable, and modifications can be saved to the database by clicking the **Save** button for that row. The frontend contains a link or button to export data from the table to a CSV file.

Let's create a mock-up from our UI. There are lots of different applications for creating mock-ups, or you could even use a pencil and paper. You can also create interactive mock-ups to demonstrate a number of functionalities. If you have done the mock-up, it is much easier to discuss requirements with the client before you start to write any actual code. With the mock-up, it is also easier for the client to understand the idea of the frontend and suggest corrections for it. Changes to the mock-up are really easy and fast to implement, compared to modifications involving actual frontend source code.

The following screenshot shows the mock-up of our car list frontend:

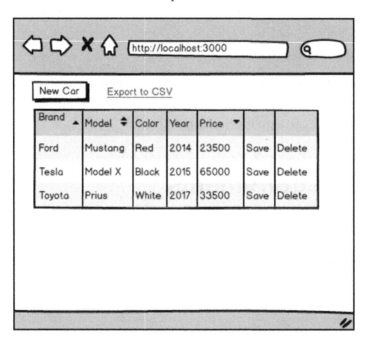

The modal form that is opened when the user presses the **New Car** button looks like the following:

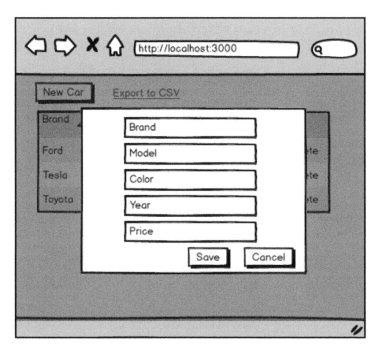

Now that we have our mock-up from our UI ready, let's look at how we can prepare our Spring Boot backend.

Preparing the Spring Boot backend

We are beginning frontend development with the unsecured version of our backend. In the first phase, we will implement all CRUD functionalities and test that these are working correctly. In the second phase, we will enable security in our backend and make the modifications that are required, and finally, we will implement authentication.

Open the Spring Boot application with Eclipse, which we created in Chapter 5, *Securing and Testing Your Backend*. Open the `SecurityConfig.java` file that defines the Spring Security configuration. Temporarily comment out the current configuration and give everyone access to all endpoints. Refer to the following modifications:

```
@Override
    protected void configure(HttpSecurity http) throws Exception {
```

```
    // Add this row to allow access to all endpoints
    http.csrf().disable().cors().and().authorizeRequests().anyRequest().permitA
    ll();
    /* Comment this out
    http.csrf().disable().cors().and().authorizeRequests()
    .antMatchers(HttpMethod.POST, "/login").permitAll()
    .anyRequest().authenticated()
    .and()
    // Filter for the api/login requests
    .addFilterBefore(new LoginFilter("/login", authenticationManager()),
    UsernamePasswordAuthenticationFilter.class)
    // Filter for other requests to check JWT in header
    .addFilterBefore(new AuthenticationFilter(),
    UsernamePasswordAuthenticationFilter.class);
    */
}
```

Now, if you run the backend and test the `http:/localhost:8080/api/cars` endpoint with Postman, you should get all cars in the response, as shown in the following screenshot:

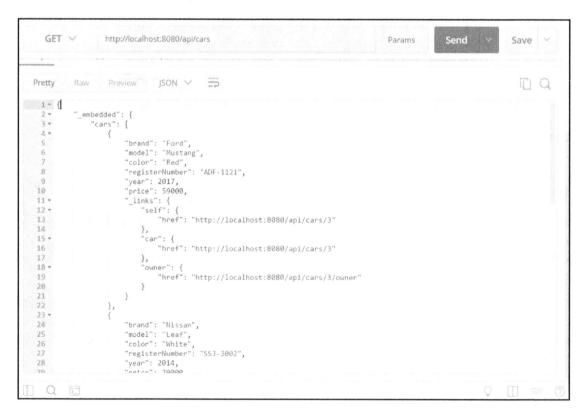

Now, we are ready to create our React project for the frontend.

Creating the React project for the frontend

Before we start coding the frontend, we have to create a new React app:

1. Open PowerShell, or any other suitable Terminal. Create a new React app by typing the following command:

    ```
    npx create-react-app carfront
    ```

2. Install the Material-UI component library by typing the following command in the project's root folder:

    ```
    npm install @material-ui/core
    ```

3. Run the app by typing the following command in the project's root folder:

    ```
    npm start
    ```

    Or, if you are using `yarn`, type in the following:

    ```
    yarn start
    ```

4. Open the `src` folder with VS Code, remove any superfluous code, and use the Material-UI `Appbar` in the `App.js` file to get the toolbar for your app. Following the modifications, your `App.js` file source code should appear as follows:

    ```
    import React from 'react';
    import './App.css';
    import AppBar from '@material-ui/core/AppBar';
    import Toolbar from '@material-ui/core/Toolbar';
    import Typography from '@material-ui/core/Typography';

    function App() {
      return (
        <div className="App">
          <AppBar position="static" color="default">
            <Toolbar>
              <Typography variant="h6" color="inherit">
                CarList
              </Typography>
            </Toolbar>
          </AppBar>
        </div>
    ```

```
   );
}

export default App;
```

And your frontend starting point will look like the following:

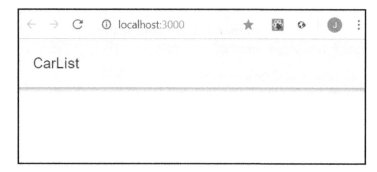

We have now created the React project for our frontend and can continue with further development.

Summary

In this chapter, we started the development of our frontend using the backend that we created in Chapter 5, *Securing and Testing Your Backend*. We defined the functionalities of the frontend and created a mock-up of the user interface. We started frontend development with an unsecured version of the backend, and we therefore made some modifications to our Spring Security configuration class. We also created the React app that we are going to use during development.

In the next chapter, we will start to add CRUD functionalities to our frontend.

Questions

1. Why should you do a mock-up of the UI?
2. How should you disable Spring Security from the backend?

Further reading

Packt has other great resources available for learning about React. These are as follows:

- *Getting Started with React*, by Doel Sengupta, Manu Singhal, et al (`https://www.packtpub.com/web-development/getting-started-react`)
- *React 16 Essentials – Second Edition*, by Adam Boduch, and Artemij Fedosejev (`https://www.packtpub.com/web-development/react-16-essentials-second-edition`)

11
Adding CRUD Functionalities

This chapter describes how we can implement CRUD functionalities to our frontend. We are going to use the components that we learned about in Chapter 9, *Useful Third-Party Components for React*. We will fetch data from our backend and present the data in a table. Then, we will implement the delete, edit, and add functionalities. In the final part of this chapter, we will add features so that we can export data to a CSV file.

In this chapter, we will cover the following topics:

- Creating the list page
- How to delete, add, and update data using the REST API
- How to show toast messages to the user
- How to export data to the CSV file from the React app

Technical requirements

The Spring Boot application that we created in Chapter 10, *Setting Up the Frontend for Our Spring Boot RESTful Web Service* (the unsecured backend), is required, as is the React app that we created in Chapter 10, *Setting Up the Frontend for Our Spring Boot RESTful Web Service* (carfront).

The following GitHub link will also be required: https://github.com/PacktPublishing/ Hands-On-Full-Stack-Development-with-Spring-Boot-2-and-React-Second-Edition/ tree/master/Chapter11.

Creating the list page

In the first phase, we will create the list page to show cars with paging, filtering, and sorting features. Run your Spring Boot backend. The cars can be fetched by sending the GET request to the http://localhost:8080/api/cars URL, as shown in Chapter 4, *Creating a RESTful Web Service with Spring Boot*.

Now, let's inspect the JSON data from the response. The array of cars can be found in the _embedded.cars node of the JSON response data:

```
GET  ∨       http://localhost:8080/api/cars

Body    Cookies (1)    Headers (9)    Test Results

Pretty    Raw    Preview    JSON ∨    ⇥

 1 ▾ {
 2 ▾     "_embedded": {
 3 ▾         "cars": [
 4 ▾             {
 5                   "brand": "Ford",
 6                   "model": "Mustang",
 7                   "color": "Red",
 8                   "registerNumber": "ADF-1121",
 9                   "year": 2017,
10                   "price": 59000,
11 ▾               "_links": {
12 ▾                   "self": {
13                           "href": "http://localhost:8080/api/cars/3"
14                       },
15 ▾                   "car": {
16                           "href": "http://localhost:8080/api/cars/3"
17                       },
18 ▾                   "owner": {
19                           "href": "http://localhost:8080/api/cars/3/owner"
20                       }
21                   }
22               },
23 ▾             {
24                   "brand": "Nissan",
25                   "model": "Leaf",
26                   "color": "White",
27                   "registerNumber": "SSJ-3002",
```

Once we know how to fetch cars from the backend, we are ready to implement the list page to show the cars. The following steps describe this in practice:

1. Open the *carfront* React app with VS Code (the React app we created in the previous chapter).

2. When the app has multiple components, it is recommended that you create a folder for them. Create a new folder called `components` in the `src` folder. With VS Code, you can create a folder by right-clicking the folder in the sidebar file explorer and selecting **New Folder** from the menu:

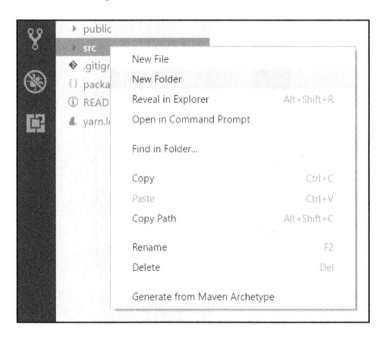

3. Create a new file called `Carlist.js` in the `components` folder. Your project structure should look like the following:

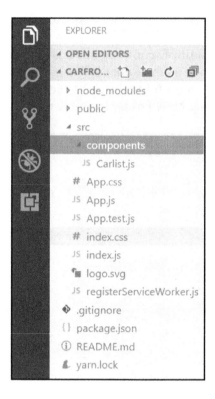

4. Open the `Carlist.js` file in the editor view and write the base code of the component, as follows:

```
import React, { Component } from 'react';

class Carlist extends Component {
  render() {
    return (
      <div></div>
    );
  }
}

export default Carlist;
```

5. We need a state for the `cars` that are fetched from the REST API. Therefore, we have to add the constructor and define a one array-type state value:

```
constructor(props) {
  super(props);
  this.state = { cars: [] };
}
```

6. Execute `fetch` in the `componentDidMount()` life cycle method. The cars from the JSON response data will be saved to the state, called `cars`:

```
componentDidMount() {
  fetch('http://localhost:8080/api/cars')
  .then((response) => response.json())
  .then((responseData) => {
    this.setState({
      cars: responseData._embedded.cars,
    });
  })
  .catch(err => console.error(err));
}
```

7. Use the `map` function to transform `car` objects into table rows in the `render()` method and add the table element:

```
render() {
 const tableRows = this.state.cars.map((car, index) =>
  <tr key={index}>
   <td>{car.brand}</td>
   <td>{car.model}</td>
   <td>{car.color}</td>
   <td>{car.year}</td>
   <td>{car.price}</td>
  </tr>
 );

 return (
 <div className="App">
  <table>
   <tbody>{tableRows}</tbody>
  </table>
 </div>
 );
}
```

8. Finally, we have to import and render the `Carlist` component in our `App.js` file. In the `App.js` file, add the `import` statement and then add the `Carlist` component to the `return` statement:

```
import React from 'react';
import './App.css';
import AppBar from '@material-ui/core/AppBar';
import Toolbar from '@material-ui/core/Toolbar';
import Typography from '@material-ui/core/Typography';
import Carlist from './components/Carlist';

function App() {
  return (
    <div className="App">
      <AppBar position="static" color="default">
        <Toolbar>
          <Typography variant="h6" color="inherit">
            CarList
          </Typography>
        </Toolbar>
      </AppBar>
      <Carlist />
    </div>
  );
}

export default App;
```

Now, if you start the React app with the `npm start` command, you should see the following list page:

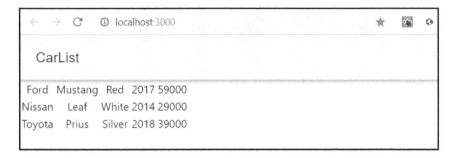

The server URL address can repeat multiple times when we create more CRUD functionalities, and it will change when the backend is deployed to a server other than the localhost. Therefore, it is better to define it as a constant. Then, when the URL value changes, we have to modify it in one place.

Let's create a new file, constants.js, in the root folder of our app:

1. Open the file in the editor and add the following line to the file:

```
export const SERVER_URL = 'http://localhost:8080/'
```

2. Then, we will import it to our Carlist.js file and use it in the fetch method:

```
//Carlist.js
// Import server url (named import)
import {SERVER_URL} from '../constants.js'

// Use imported constant in the fetch method
fetch(SERVER_URL + 'api/cars')
```

3. Finally, your Carlist.js file source code should appear as follows:

```
import React, { Component } from 'react';
import {SERVER_URL} from '../constants.js'

class Carlist extends Component {
  constructor(props) {
    super(props);
    this.state = { cars: []};
  }

  componentDidMount() {
    fetch(SERVER_URL + 'api/cars')
    .then((response) => response.json())
    .then((responseData) => {
      this.setState({
```

```
                  cars: responseData._embedded.cars,
                });
              })
              .catch(err => console.error(err));
          }
        render() {
          const tableRows = this.state.cars.map((car, index) =>
            <tr key={index}><td>{car.brand}</td>
             <td>{car.model}</td><td>{car.color}</td>
             <td>{car.year}</td><td>{car.price}</td></tr>);

          return (
            <div className="App">
              <table><tbody>{tableRows}</tbody></table>
            </div>
          );
        }
      }

      export default Carlist;
```

Now, we will use React Table to get the paging, filtering, and sorting features out of the box. Stop the development server by pressing *Ctrl + C* in the Terminal and type the following command to install React Table. Post installation, restart the app:

```
npm install react-table
```

Then, import react-table and the style sheet to your Carlist.js file:

```
import ReactTable from "react-table";
import 'react-table/react-table.css';
```

Then, remove table and tableRows from the render() method. The data prop of React Table is this.state.cars, which contains fetched cars. We also have to define the columns of the table, where accessor is the field of the car object and header is the text of the header. To enable filtering, we set the filterable prop of the table to true. Refer to the source code of the following render() method:

```
render() {
  const columns = [{
    Header: 'Brand',
    accessor: 'brand'
  }, {
    Header: 'Model',
    accessor: 'model',
  }, {
    Header: 'Color',
```

```
      accessor: 'color',
    }, {
      Header: 'Year',
      accessor: 'year',
    }, {
      Header: 'Price €',
      accessor: 'price',
    },]

    return (
      <div className="App">
        <ReactTable data={this.state.cars} columns={columns}
          filterable={true}/>
      </div>
    );
}
```

With the React Table component, we acquired all the necessary features for our table with a small amount of coding. Now, the list page looks like the following:

Next, we will implement the delete functionality.

The delete functionality

Items can be deleted from the database by sending the DELETE method request to the `http://localhost:8080/api/cars/[carid]` endpoint. If we look at the JSON response data, we can see that each car contains a link to itself and that it can be accessed from the `_links.self.href` node, as shown in the following screenshot:

The following steps demonstrate how to implement the delete functionality:

1. Here, we will create a button for each row in the table. The accessor of the button will be `_links.self.href`, which we can use to call the delete function that we will create soon. But first, add a new column to the table using `Cell` to render the button. Refer to the following source code. We don't want to enable sorting and filtering for the button column. Therefore, these props are set to `false`. The button invokes the `onDelClick` function when pressed and sends a link to the car as an argument:

```
const columns = [{
  Header: 'Brand',
  accessor: 'brand'
}, {
  Header: 'Model',
  accessor: 'model',
}, {
  Header: 'Color',
  accessor: 'color',
}, {
  Header: 'Year',
  accessor: 'year',
}, {
  Header: 'Price €',
  accessor: 'price',
}, {
  id: 'delbutton',
  sortable: false,
  filterable: false,
  width: 100,
  accessor: '_links.self.href',
  Cell: ({value}) => (<button
onClick={()=>{this.onDelClick(value)}}>Delete</button>)
}]
```

2. Implement the `onDelClick` function. But first, let's take the `fetchCars` function out of the `componentDidMount()` method. This is necessary because we also want to call the `fetchCars` function after the car has been deleted in order to show an updated list of cars to the user. Create a new function called `fetchCars()` and copy the code from the `componentDidMount()` method into a new function. Then, call the `fetchCars()` function from the `componentDidMount()` function to fetch cars:

```
componentDidMount() {
  this.fetchCars();
```

```
      }

      fetchCars = () => {
        fetch(SERVER_URL + 'api/cars')
        .then((response) => response.json())
        .then((responseData) => {
          this.setState({
            cars: responseData._embedded.cars,
          });
        })
        .catch(err => console.error(err));
      }
```

3. Implement the `onDelClick` function. We send the DELETE request to a car link, and when the DELETE request succeeds, we refresh the list page by calling the `fetchCars()` function:

```
      // Delete car
      onDelClick = (link) => {
        fetch(link, {method: 'DELETE'})
        .then(res => this.fetchCars())
        .catch(err => console.error(err))
      }
```

When you start your app, the frontend should look like the following screenshot. The car disappears from the list when the **Delete** button is pressed:

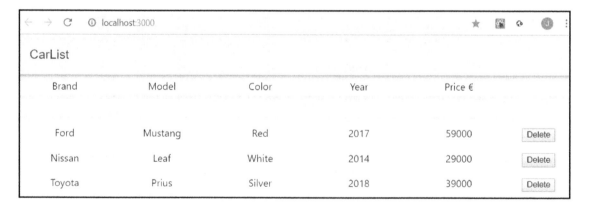

It would be nice to show the user some feedback in the event of successful deletion, or if there are any errors. Let's implement a toast message to show the status of deletion. For that, we are going to use the `react-toastify` component (https://github.com/fkhadra/react-toastify). Install the component by typing the following command into the Terminal you are using:

```
npm install react-toastify
```

Once installation is complete, start your app and open the `Carlist.js` file in the editor. We have to import `ToastContainer`, `toast`, and the style sheet so that we can start using `react-toastify`. Add the following import statements to your `Carlist.js` file:

```
import { ToastContainer, toast } from 'react-toastify';
import 'react-toastify/dist/ReactToastify.css';
```

`ToastContainer` is the container component for showing toast messages, and it should be inside the `render()` method. In `ToastContainer`, you can define the duration of the toast message in milliseconds using the `autoClose` prop. Add the `ToastContainer` component inside the return statement in the `render()` method, just after `ReactTable`:

```
return (
  <div className="App">
    <ReactTable data={this.state.cars} columns={columns}
      filterable={true}/>
    <ToastContainer autoClose={1500} } />
  </div>
);
```

Then, we will call the `toast` method in the `onDelClick()` function to show the toast message. You can define the type and position of the message. The `success` message is shown when deletion succeeds, and the `error` message is shown in the case of an `error`:

```
// Delete car
onDelClick = (link) => {
  fetch(link, {method: 'DELETE'})
  .then(res => {
    toast.success("Car deleted", {
      position: toast.POSITION.BOTTOM_LEFT
    });
    this.fetchCars();
  })
  .catch(err => {
    toast.error("Error when deleting", {
      position: toast.POSITION.BOTTOM_LEFT
    });
    console.error(err)
```

```
    })
  }
```

Now, you will see the toast message when the car is deleted, as shown in the following screenshot:

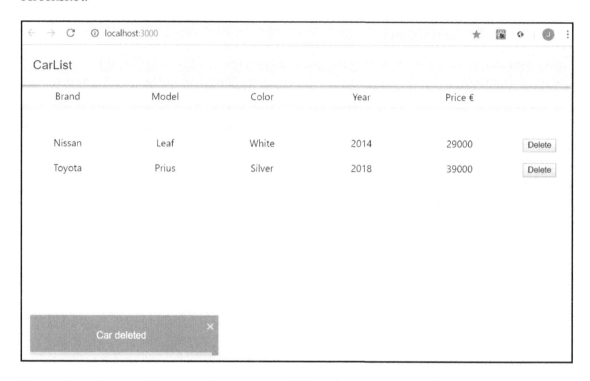

To avoid accidental deletion of the car, it would be nice to have a confirmation dialog after the delete button has been pressed. We will implement this using the window object's `confirm` method. Add `confirm` to the `onDelClick` method:

```
// Delete car
onDelClick = (link) => {
  if (window.confirm('Are you sure to delete?')) {
    fetch(link, {method: 'DELETE'})
    .then(res => {
      toast.success("Car deleted", {
        position: toast.POSITION.BOTTOM_LEFT
      });
      this.fetchCars();
    })
    .catch(err => {
      toast.error("Error when deleting", {
```

```
      position: toast.POSITION.BOTTOM_LEFT
    });
    console.error(err)
  })
  }
}
```

If you press the **Delete** button now, the confirmation dialog will be opened and the car will only be deleted if you press the **OK** button:

Next, we will begin implementation of the functionality to add a new car.

The add functionality

The next step is to create an add functionality for the frontend. We will implement this using the Material-UI modal dialog. We already went through the utilization of Material-UI modal form in `Chapter 9`, *Useful Third-Party React Components for React*. We will add the **New Car** button to the user interface, which opens the modal form when it is pressed. The modal form contains all the fields that are required to save the car, as well as the button for saving and canceling.

We already installed the Material-UI component library to our frontend app in `Chapter 10`, *Setting Up the Frontend for Our Spring Boot RESTful Web Service*.

The following steps show you how to create add functionality using the modal dialog component:

1. Create a new file called AddCar.js in the components folder and write some function-class base code to the file, as shown here. Add the imports for the Material-UI Dialog component:

```
import React from 'react';
import Dialog from '@material-ui/core/Dialog';
import DialogActions from '@material-ui/core/DialogActions';
import DialogContent from '@material-ui/core/DialogContent';
import DialogContentText from '@material-
ui/core/DialogContentText';
import DialogTitle from '@material-ui/core/DialogTitle';

const AddCar = (props) => {
  return (
    <div>
    </div>
  );
};

export default AddCar;
```

2. Introduce an object typed state that contains all car fields using the useState hook. For the dialog, we also need a Boolean typed state to define the visibility of the dialog form:

```
import React, { useState } from 'react';
import Dialog from '@material-ui/core/Dialog';
import DialogActions from '@material-ui/core/DialogActions';
import DialogContent from '@material-ui/core/DialogContent';
import DialogTitle from '@material-ui/core/DialogTitle';

const AddCar = (props) => {
  const [open, setOpen] = useState(false);
  const [car, setCar] = useState({
    brand: '', model: '', color: '', year: '', fuel:'', price: ''
  });

  return (
    <div>
    </div>
  );
};

export default AddCar;
```

3. Add a dialog form inside the `return` statement. The form contains the `Dialog` Material-UI component with buttons and the input fields that are required to collect the car data. The button that opens the modal window, which will be shown in the car list page, must be outside of the `Dialog` component. All input fields should have the `name` attribute with a value that is the same as the name of the state the value will be saved to. Input fields also have the `onChange` handler, which saves the value to state by invoking the `handleChange` function. The `handleClose` and `handleOpen` functions set the value of the `open` state, which affects the visibility of the modal form:

```
const [open, setOpen] = useState(false);
const [car, setCar] = useState({
  brand: '', model: '', color: '', year: '', fuel:'', price: ''
});

// Open the modal form
const handleClickOpen = () => {
 setOpen(true);
};

// Close the modal form
const handleClose = () => {
 setOpen(false);
};

const handleChange = (event) => {
 setCar({...car, [event.target.name]: event.target.value});
}

return (
 <div>
   <button style={{margin: 10}} onClick={handleClickOpen}>New
Car</button>
   <Dialog open={open} onClose={handleClose}>
     <DialogTitle>New car</DialogTitle>
     <DialogContent>
       <input type="text" placeholder="Brand" name="brand"
         value={car.brand} onChange={handleChange}/><br/>
       <input type="text" placeholder="Model" name="model"
         value={car.model} onChange={handleChange}/><br/>
       <input type="text" placeholder="Color" name="color"
         value={car.color} onChange={handleChange}/><br/>
       <input type="text" placeholder="Year" name="year"
         value={car.year} onChange={handleChange}/><br/>
       <input type="text" placeholder="Price" name="price"
         value={car.price} onChange={handleChange}/><br/>
```

```
      </DialogContent>
      <DialogActions>
        <button onClick={handleClose}>Cancel</button>
        <button onClick={handleClose}>Save</button>
      </DialogActions>
    </Dialog>
  </div>
);
```

4. Implement the `addCar` function to the `Carlist.js` file, which will send the POST request to the backend `api/cars` endpoint. The request will include the new `car` object inside the body and the `'Content-Type'`: `'application/json'` header. The header is required because the `car` object is converted into JSON format using the `JSON.stringify()` method:

```
// Add new car
addCar(car) {
  fetch(SERVER_URL + 'api/cars',
    { method: 'POST',
      headers: {
        'Content-Type': 'application/json',
      },
      body: JSON.stringify(car)
    })
  .then(res => this.fetchCars())
  .catch(err => console.error(err))
}
```

5. Import the `AddCar` component into the `Carlist.js` file:

```
import AddCar from './AddCar';
```

6. Add the `AddCar` component to the `Carlist.js` file's `render()` method and pass the `addCar` and `fetchCars` functions as props to the `AddCar` component. This allows us to call these functions from the `AddCar` component. Now, the return statement of the `CarList.js` file should appear as follows:

```
// Carlist.js
return (
  <div className="App">
    <AddCar addCar={this.addCar} fetchCars={this.fetchCars} />
    <ReactTable data={this.state.cars} columns={columns}
      filterable={true} pageSize={10}/>
    <ToastContainer autoClose={1500}/>
  </div>
);
```

7. If you start the frontend app, it should now look like the following, and if you press the **New Car** button, it should open the modal form:

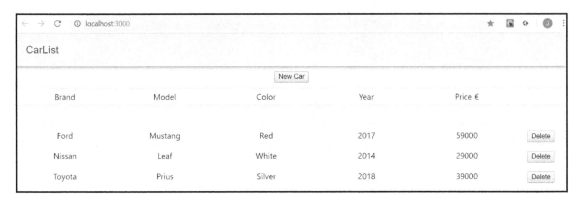

8. Create a function called `handleSave` in the `AddCar.js` file. The `handleSave` function calls the `addCar` function, which can be accessed using props, and pass the car state object to it. Finally, the modal form is closed and the car list is updated:

```
// Save car and close modal form
const handleSave = () => {
  props.addCar(car);
  handleClose();
}
```

9. Finally, you have to change the button's `onClick` to call the `handleSave` function, `onClick={handleSave}`. Now, you can open the modal form by pressing the **New Car** button. Then, you can fill the form with data and press the **Save** button. At this point, the form doesn't have a nice appearance, but we are going to style it in the next chapter:

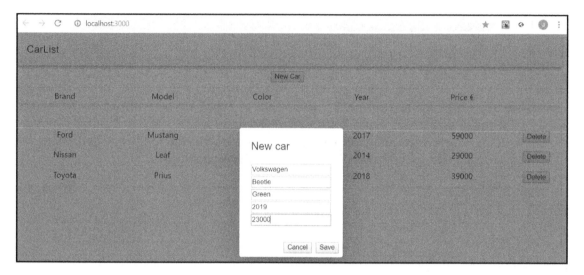

The list page is refreshed, and the new car can be seen in the list:

Next, we will begin to implement edit functionality in relation to our frontend.

The edit functionality

We will implement the edit functionality by adding the **Edit** button to each table row.
When the row edit button is pressed, it opens the modal form, where the user can edit the
existing car and finally save their changes:

1. First, we will create a skeleton of the EditCar component, which will be the
   form for editing an existing car. Create a new file called EditCar.js in the
   components folder. The EditCar component code is similar to the AddCar
   component, but for now, in the handleSave function, we should call the update
   function that we will implement later:

```
import React, { useState } from 'react';
import Dialog from '@material-ui/core/Dialog';
import DialogActions from '@material-ui/core/DialogActions';
import DialogContent from '@material-ui/core/DialogContent';
import DialogTitle from '@material-ui/core/DialogTitle';

const EditCar = (props) => {
  const [open, setOpen] = useState(false);
  const [car, setCar] = useState({brand: '', model: '', year: '',
color: '', price: ''});

  const handleClickOpen = () => {
    setOpen(true);
  };

  const handleClose = () => {
    setOpen(false);
  };

  const handleChange = (event) => {
    setCar({...car, [event.target.name]: event.target.value});
  }

  // Update car and close modal form
  const handleSave = () => {
  }

  return (
    <div>
      <button onClick={handleClickOpen}>Edit</button>
      <Dialog open={open} onClose={handleClose}>
        <DialogTitle>Edit car</DialogTitle>
        <DialogContent>
          <input type="text" placeholder="Brand" name="brand"
```

```
                   value={car.brand} onChange={handleChange}/><br/>
             <input type="text" placeholder="Model" name="model"
                value={car.model} onChange={handleChange}/><br/>
             <input type="text" placeholder="Color" name="color"
                value={car.color} onChange={handleChange}/><br/>
             <input type="text" placeholder="Year" name="year"
                value={car.year} onChange={handleChange}/><br/>
             <input type="text" placeholder="Price" name="price"
                value={car.price} onChange={handleChange}/><br/>
          </DialogContent>
          <DialogActions>
            <button onClick={handleClose}>Cancel</button>
            <button onClick={handleSave}>Save</button>
          </DialogActions>
          </Dialog>
       </div>
    );
  };

    export default EditCar;
```

2. To update the car data, we have to send the PUT request to the
   http://localhost:8080/api/cars/[carid] URL. The link will be the same
   as it is for the delete functionality. The request contains the updated car object
   inside the body, and the 'Content-Type': 'application/json' header that
   we had in the add functionality. Create a new function called updateCar in the
   Carlist.js file. The source code of the function is shown in the following code
   snippet. The function gets two arguments—the updated car object and the
   request URL. Following a successful update, we will show a toast message to the
   user:

```
// Carlist.js file
// Update car
updateCar(car, link) {
  fetch(link,
  { method: 'PUT',
    headers: {
      'Content-Type': 'application/json',
    },
    body: JSON.stringify(car)
  })
  .then(res => {
    toast.success("Changes saved", {
      position: toast.POSITION.BOTTOM_LEFT
    });
    this.fetchCars();
```

```
    })
    .catch(err =>
      toast.error("Error when saving", {
        position: toast.POSITION.BOTTOM_LEFT
      })
    )
  }
```

3. Next, we will import the `EditCar` component into the `CarList` component so
   that we are able to show it in the car list. Add the following import to
   the `CarList.js` file:

   ```
   import EditCar from './EditCar';
   ```

4. Now, add the `EditCar` component to the table columns in the same way that we
   did with the delete functionality. Now, the `EditCar` component is rendered to
   table cells and it only shows the **Edit** button. This is because the modal form is
   not visible before the button is pressed. When the user presses the **Edit** button, it
   sets the `open` state value to `true` in the `EditCar` component, and the modal form
   is shown. We pass four `props` to the `EditCar` component. The first props is `row`,
   which contains all the values from the row as an `object` (=car object). The
   second argument is `value`, which is set to be `_links.href.self`, which will be
   the URL of the car that we need in the request. The third one is the `updateCar`
   function, which we have to call from the `EditCar` component in order to be able
   to save changes. The last one is the `fetchCars` function which is used for
   refreshing the car list following an update:

   ```
   const columns = [{
       Header: 'Brand',
       accessor: 'brand'
     }, {
       Header: 'Model',
       accessor: 'model'
     }, {
       Header: 'Color',
       accessor: 'color'
     }, {
       Header: 'Year',
       accessor: 'year'
     }, {
       Header: 'Fuel',
       accessor: 'fuel'
     }, {
       Header: 'Price (€)',
       accessor: 'price'
   ```

```
      }, {
        sortable: false,
        filterable: false,
        width: 100,
        accessor: '_links.self.href',
        Cell: ({value, row}) => (<EditCar car={row} link={value}
          updateCar={this.updateCar} fetchCars={this.fetchCars} />),
        width: 100
      }, {
        sortable: false,
        filterable: false,
        width: 100,
        accessor: '_links.self.href',
        Cell: ({value}) => (<button
onClick={()=>{this.onDelClick(value)}}>Delete</button>)
      }]
```

5. Next, we will perform the final modifications to the EditCar.js file. We get the car to be edited from the car props, which we use to populate the form with the existing car values. Change the handleClickOpen function in the EditCar.js file. Now, when the form is opened, the car state is updated with the values from the car props:

```
      const handleClickOpen = () => {
        setCar({brand: props.car.brand, model: props.car.model, color:
props.car.color,
          year: props.car.year, fuel: props.car.fuel, price:
props.car.price })
        setOpen(true);
      }
```

6. Finally, we will change the handleSave function and call the updateCar function using props:

```
      // Update car and close modal form
      const handleSave = () => {
        props.updateCar(car, props.link);
        handleClose();
      }
```

7. If you press the **Edit** button in the table, it opens the modal edit form and shows the car from that row. The updated values are saved to the database when you press the **Save** button:

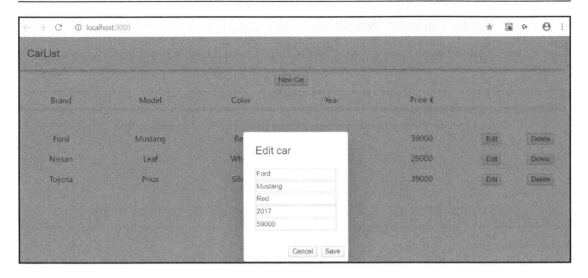

Now, we have implemented all CRUD functionalities in relation to our frontend. In Chapter 12, *Styling the Frontend with React Material-UI*, we will focus on styling the frontend.

Other functionalities

One feature that we will also implement is a **Comma-Separated Values** (CSV) export of the data. There's a package called react-csv (https://github.com/abdennour/react-csv) that can be used to export an array of data to the CSV file.

If your app is running, stop the development server by pressing *Ctrl* + *C* in the Terminal, and type the following command to install react-csv. Post installation, restart the app:

```
npm install react-csv
```

The react-csv package contains two components—CSVLink and CSVDownload. We will use the first one in our app, so add the following import to the Carlist.js file:

```
import { CSVLink } from 'react-csv';
```

The CSVLink component takes the data prop, which contains the data array that will be exported to the CSV file. You can also define the data separator using the separator prop (the default separator is a comma). Add the CSVLink component inside the return statement in the render() method.

The value of the `data` prop will now be `this.state.cars`:

```
// Carlist.js render() method
return (
  <div className="App">
    <AddCar addCar={this.addCar} fetchCars={this.fetchCars} />
    <CSVLink data={this.state.cars} separator=";">Export CSV</CSVLink>
    <ReactTable data={this.state.cars} columns={columns}
      filterable={true}/>
    <ToastContainer autoClose={1500} />
  </div>
);
```

Open the app in your browser. You should see the **Export CSV** link in your app. The styling is not nice, but we will handle that in the next chapter. If you press the link, you will get the data in the CSV file:

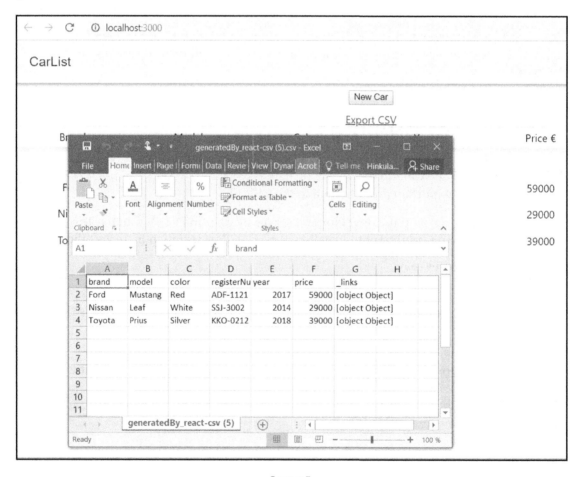

Now, all the functionalities have been implemented.

Summary

In this chapter, we implemented all the functionalities for our app. We started with fetching the cars from the backend and showing these in React Table, which provides paging, sorting, and filtering features. Then, we implemented the delete functionality and used the toast component to give feedback to the user.

The add and edit functionalities were implemented using the Material-UI modal dialog component. Finally, we implemented the ability to export data to a CSV file.

In the next chapter, we are going to style our frontend using the React Material-UI component library.

Questions

1. How do you fetch and present data using the REST API with React?
2. How would you delete data using the REST API with React?
3. How do you add data using the REST API with React?
4. How would you update data using the REST API with React?
5. How do you show toast messages with React?
6. How would you export data to a CSV file with React?

Further reading

Packt has other great resources available for learning about React. These are as follows:

- *Getting Started with React*, by Doel Sengupta, Manu Singhal, and et al (`https://www.packtpub.com/web-development/getting-started-react`)
- *React 16 Essentials – Second Edition*, by Adam Boduch, and Artemij Fedosejev (`https://www.packtpub.com/web-development/react-16-essentials-second-edition`)

Styling the Frontend with React Material-UI

12

This chapter explains how to use Material-UI components in our frontend. We will use the `Button` component to show the styled buttons. The modal form input fields are replaced by `TextField` components, which have many nice features. We will also use the Material-UI `Grid` component, which provides a responsive grid layout.

In this chapter, we will cover the following topics:

- Using the Material-UI `Button` component in our frontend
- Using the Material-UI `Grid` component in our frontend
- Using the Material-UI `TextField` component in our frontend

Technical requirements

The Spring Boot application that we created in Chapter 5, *Securing and Testing Your Backend*, is required, together with the modification from Chapter 10, *Setting Up the Frontend for Our Spring Boot RESTful Web Service* (the unsecured backend).

We also need the React app that we used in Chapter 11, *Adding CRUD Functionalities* (*carfront*).

The following code samples available at the GitHub link will also be required: https://github.com/PacktPublishing/Hands-On-Full-Stack-Development-with-Spring-Boot-2-and-React-Second-Edition/tree/master/Chapter12.

Using the Button component

Let's first change all the buttons to use the Material-UI `Button` component. Import `Button` to the `AddCar.js` file:

```
// AddCar.js
import Button from '@material-ui/core/Button';
```

Change the buttons to use the `Button` component. In the list page, we are using the outlined button and in the modal form, we use buttons without any borders. The following code shows the `AddCar` component:

```
return (
    <div>
      <Button variant="outlined" color="primary" style={{margin: 10}}
onClick={handleClickOpen}>
        New Car
      </Button>
      <Dialog open={open} onClose={handleClose}>
          <DialogTitle>New car</DialogTitle>
          <DialogContent>
            <input type="text" placeholder="Brand" name="brand"
              value={car.brand} onChange={handleChange}/><br/>
            <input type="text" placeholder="Model" name="model"
              value={car.model} onChange={handleChange}/><br/>
            <input type="text" placeholder="Color" name="color"
              value={car.color} onChange={handleChange}/><br/>
            <input type="text" placeholder="Year" name="year"
              value={car.year} onChange={handleChange}/><br/>
            <input type="text" placeholder="Price" name="price"
              value={car.price} onChange={handleChange}/><br/>
          </DialogContent>
          <DialogActions>
            <Button color="secondary" onClick={handleClose}>Cancel</Button>
            <Button color="primary" onClick={handleSave}>Save</Button>
          </DialogActions>
      </Dialog>
    </div>
  );
```

Now, the list page button should look like the following:

And the modal form buttons should look like the following:

We also need to change the buttons in the `EditCar` component. The button that opens the modal form is the **Edit** button, which is shown in the table. Therefore, we use the button without borders and set the size to small. Refer to the following source code of the `EditCar` component:

```
return (
  <div>
    <Button color="primary" size="small"
onClick={handleClickOpen}>Edit</Button>
    <Dialog open={open} onClose={handleClose}>
        <DialogTitle>Edit car</DialogTitle>
        <DialogContent>
          <input type="text" placeholder="Brand" name="brand"
            value={car.brand} onChange={handleChange}/><br/>
            <input type="text" placeholder="Model" name="model"
              value={car.model} onChange={handleChange}/><br/>
            <input type="text" placeholder="Color" name="color"
              value={car.color} onChange={handleChange}/><br/>
            <input type="text" placeholder="Year" name="year"
              value={car.year} onChange={handleChange}/><br/>
            <input type="text" placeholder="Price" name="price"
              value={car.price} onChange={handleChange}/><br/>
```

```
        </DialogContent>
        <DialogActions>
            <Button color="secondary" onClick={handleClose}>Cancel</Button>
            <Button color="primary" onClick={handleSave}>Save</Button>
        </DialogActions>
      </Dialog>
  </div>
);
```

We also use the `Button` component in the car table and define the button size as small for the `Delete` button in `carlist.js`. Refer to the following source code for the table columns:

```
// Carlist.js render() method
const columns = [{
    Header: 'Brand',
    accessor: 'brand'
  }, {
    Header: 'Model',
    accessor: 'model',
  }, {
    Header: 'Color',
    accessor: 'color',
  }, {
    Header: 'Year',
    accessor: 'year',
  }, {
    Header: 'Price €',
    accessor: 'price',
  }, {
    sortable: false,
    filterable: false,
    width: 100,
    accessor: '_links.self.href',
    Cell: ({value, row}) => (<EditCar car={row} link={value}
updateCar={this.updateCar}
            fetchCars={this.fetchCars} />),
  }, {
    sortable: false,
    filterable: false,
    width: 100,
    accessor: '_links.self.href',
    Cell: ({value}) => (<Button size="small" color="secondary"
        onClick={()=>{this.onDelClick(value)}}>Delete</Button>)
  }]
```

Now, the table should look like the following:

Brand	Model	Color	Year	Price €		
Ford	Mustang	Red	2017	59000	EDIT	DELETE
Nissan	Leaf	White	2014	29000	EDIT	DELETE
Toyota	Prius	Silver	2018	39000	EDIT	DELETE

The table is now ready, with the styled buttons and the filtering and sorting functionalities.

Using the Grid component

Material-UI provides a `Grid` component that can be used to get a grid layout to your React app. We will use `Grid` to get the **New Item** button and the **Export CSV** link on the same line.

Add the following import to the `Carlist.js` file to import the `Grid` component:

```
import Grid from '@material-ui/core/Grid';
```

Next, we wrap `AddCar` and `CSVLink` inside the `Grid` components. There are two types of `Grid` components—a container and an item. `AddCar` and `CSVLink` are wrapped inside the item type `Grid` components. Then, both item `Grid` components are wrapped inside the container type `Grid` component:

```
// Carlist.js render() method
return (
  <div className="App">
    <Grid container>
      <Grid item>
        <AddCar addCar={this.addCar} fetchCars={this.fetchCars} />
      </Grid>
      <Grid item style={{padding: 15}}>
        <CSVLink data={this.state.cars} separator=";">Export CSV</CSVLink>
      </Grid>
    </Grid>
    <ReactTable data={this.state.cars} columns={columns}
        filterable={true}/>
    <ToastContainer autoClose={1500} />
  </div>
);
```

Now, your app should look like the following:

The button and CSV link are now placed in one row.

Using the TextField components

In this section, we'll change the text input in the modal form using the Material-UI
`TextField` component. Add the following import statement to the `AddCar.js` and
`EditCar.js` files:

```
import TextField from '@material-ui/core/TextField';
```

Then, change the input to the `TextField` components in the add and edit forms. We are
using the `label` props to set the labels of the `TextField` components. The first `TextField`
component contains `autoFocus` props, and the input will be focused on this field:

```
return (
  <div>
    <Button variant="outlined" color="primary" style={{margin: 10}}
onClick={handleClickOpen}>
      New Car
    </Button>
    <Dialog open={open} onClose={handleClose}>
        <DialogTitle>New car</DialogTitle>
        <DialogContent>
          <TextField autoFocus fullWidth label="Brand" name="brand"
              value={car.brand} onChange={handleChange}/>
          <TextField fullWidth label="Model" name="model"
              value={car.model} onChange={handleChange}/>
          <TextField fullWidth label="Color" name="color"
```

```
                value={car.color} onChange={handleChange}/>
            <TextField fullWidth label="Year" name="year"
                value={car.year} onChange={handleChange}/>
            <TextField fullWidth label="Price" name="price"
                value={car.price} onChange={handleChange}/>
        </DialogContent>
        <DialogActions>
            <Button color="secondary" onClick={handleClose}>Cancel</Button>
            <Button color="primary" onClick={handleSave}>Save</Button>
        </DialogActions>
    </Dialog>
  </div>
);
```

After the modifications, the modal form should look like the following:

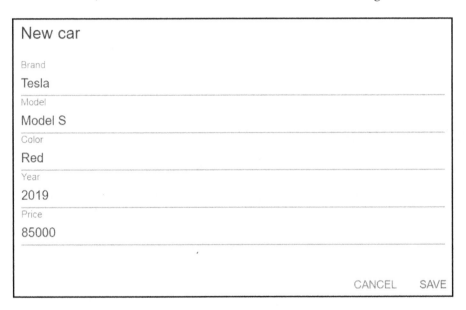

Now, we have completed the styling of our frontend using Material-UI components.

Summary

In this chapter, we finalized our frontend using Material-UI. Material-UI is the React component library that implements Google's Material Design. We replaced all the buttons with the Material-UI `Button` components.

Our modal form got a new look by using the Material-UI `TextField` component. After these modifications, our frontend looks more professional and uniform.

In the next chapter, we will focus on frontend testing.

Questions

1. What is Material-UI?
2. How should you use different Material-UI components?
3. How should you remove unused components?

Further reading

Packt has other great resources available for learning about React. These are as follows:

- *Getting Started with React*, by Doel Sengupta, Manu Singhal, Et al (`https://www.packtpub.com/web-development/getting-started-react`)
- *React 16 Essentials – Second Edition*, by Adam Boduch and Artemij Fedosejev (`https://www.packtpub.com/web-development/react-16-essentials-second-edition`)

13
Testing Your Frontend

This chapter explains the basics of testing React apps. It will give us an overview of using Jest, which is a JavaScript test library developed by Facebook. We will cover Enzyme, which is a testing utility for React, developed by Airbnb. We will look at how you can create new test suites and tests, and also how to run the test and work with the results.

In this chapter, we will cover the following topics:

- Using Jest
- Snapshot testing
- Using Enzyme

Technical requirements

The Spring Boot application that we created in Chapter 5, *Securing and Testing Your Backend*, is required (GitHub: `https://github.com/PacktPublishing/Hands-On-Full-Stack-Development-with-Spring-Boot-2-and-React-Second-Edition/tree/master/Chapter05`), as is the React app that we used in Chapter 12, *Styling the Frontend with React Material-UI* (GitHub: `https://github.com/PacktPublishing/Hands-On-Full-Stack-Development-with-Spring-Boot-2-and-React-Second-Edition/tree/master/Chapter12`).

The code samples available at the following GitHub link will also be required to follow along with this chapter: `https://github.com/PacktPublishing/Hands-On-Full-Stack-Development-with-Spring-Boot-2-and-React-Second-Edition/tree/master/Chapter13`.

Using Jest

Jest is a test library for JavaScript developed by Facebook (`https://jestjs.io/`). Jest is widely used with React and provides lots of useful features for testing. You can create a snapshot test, where you can take snapshots from React trees and investigate how states are changing. Jest also has mock functionalities that you can use to test, for example, your asynchronous REST API calls. Jest also provides functions that are required for the assertions in your test cases.

We will first see how you can create a simple test case for a basic JavaScript function that performs some simple calculations. The following function takes two numbers as arguments and returns the product of the numbers:

```
// multi.js
export const calcMulti = (x, y) => {
    x * y;
}
```

The following code shows a Jest test for the preceding function. The test case starts with a `test` method that runs the test case. The `test` method has an alias, called `it`, which we will use in the React examples later. The test method gets the two required arguments—the test name and the function that contains the test. `expect` is used when you want to test values. The `toBe` function is the so-called matcher that checks whether the result from the function equals the value in the matcher. There are many different matchers available in Jest and you can find these from their documentation:

```
// multi.test.js
import {calcMulti} from './multi';

test('2 * 3 equals 6', () => {
  expect(calcMulti(2, 3)).toBe(6);
});
```

Jest comes with `create-react-app`, so we don't have to do any installations or configurations to start testing. It is recommended to create a folder called _test_ for your test files. The test files should have the `.test.js` extension. If you look at your React frontend in the VS Code file explorer, you can see that in the `src` folder, there is already one test file automatically created, and it is called `App.test.js`:

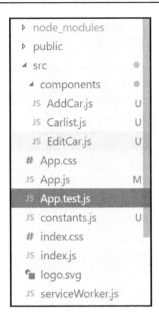

The source code of the `test` file is as follows:

```
import React from 'react';
import ReactDOM from 'react-dom';
import App from './App';

it('renders without crashing', () => {
  const div = document.createElement('div');
  ReactDOM.render(<App />, div);
  ReactDOM.unmountComponentAtNode(div);
});
```

The following `test` file creates a `div` element to the DOM and mounts the `App` component to it. Finally, the component is unmounted from `div`. So, it just tests that your `App` component can be rendered and that the test runner is working. `it` is an alias for the `test` function in Jest; the first argument is the name of the test; and the second argument is the function that is executed and tested.

You can run your tests by typing the following command into your Terminal:

npm test

Or, if you are using Yarn, type the following:

yarn test

After your tests have been executed, and everything is working correctly, you will see the following information in the Terminal:

```
PASS  src\App.test.js
  √ renders without crashing (156ms)

Test Suites: 1 passed, 1 total
Tests:       1 passed, 1 total
Snapshots:   0 total
Time:        3.623s
Ran all test suites related to changed files.
```

We have now executed our first test case and it has passed.

Snapshot testing

Snapshot testing is a useful tool to test that there are no unwanted changes in your user interface. Jest generates snapshot files when the snapshot tests are executed. The next time the tests are executed, the new snapshot is compared to the previous one. If there are changes between the content of the files, the test case fails and an error message is shown in the Terminal.

To start snapshot testing, perform the following steps:

1. Install the `react-test-renderer` package. The `--save-dev` parameter means that this dependency is saved to the `package.json` file's `devDependencies` part and it is only used for development purposes. If you type the `npm install --production` command in the installation phase, dependencies in the `devDependencies` part are not installed. So, all dependencies that are only required in the development phase should be installed using the `--save-dev` parameter:

   ```
   npm install react-test-renderer --save-dev
   ```

2. Your `package.json` file should appear as follows once the new `devDependecies` part has been added to the file:

   ```
   {
     "name": "carfront",
     "version": "0.1.0",
     "private": true,
     "dependencies": {
       "@material-ui/core": "^3.9.3",
   ```

```
    "react": "^16.8.6",
    "react-csv": "^1.1.1",
    "react-dom": "^16.8.6",
    "react-scripts": "2.1.8",
    "react-table": "^6.9.2",
    "react-toastify": "^5.0.1"
  },
  "scripts": {
    "start": "react-scripts start",
    "build": "react-scripts build",
    "test": "react-scripts test",
    "eject": "react-scripts eject"
  },
  "eslintConfig": {
    "extends": "react-app"
  },
  "browserslist": [
    ">0.2%",
    "not dead",
    "not ie <= 11",
    "not op_mini all"
  ],
  "devDependencies": {
    "react-test-renderer": "^16.8.6"
  }
}
```

3. Import `TestRenderer` to your test file:

```
import TestRenderer from 'react-test-renderer';
```

Let's now add a new snapshot test case to our `App.test.js` file. The test case will create a snapshot test of our `AddCar` component:

1. Import the `AddCar` component to our test file:

```
import AddCar from './components/AddCar';
```

2. Add the following test code after the first test case, which already exists in the file. The test case takes a snapshot from our `App` component and then compares whether the snapshot differs from the previous snapshot:

```
it('renders a snapshot', () => {
  const tree = TestRenderer.create(<AddCar/>).toJSON();
  expect(tree).toMatchSnapshot();
});
```

3. Run the test cases again by typing the following command in your Terminal:

```
npm test
```

4. Now, you can see the following message in the Terminal. The test suite tells us the number of test files, and the tests tell us the number of test cases:

```
PASS  src/App.test.jstal
  √ renders without crashing (208ms)
  √ renders a snapshot (30ms)

  › 1 snapshot written.
Snapshot Summary
  › 1 snapshot written from 1 test suite.

Test Suites: 1 passed, 1 total
Tests:       2 passed, 2 total
Snapshots:   1 written, 1 total
Time:        5.548s
```

When the test is executed for the first time, a _snapshots_ folder is created. This folder contains all the snapshot files that are generated from the test cases. Now, you can see that there is one snapshot file generated, as shown in the following screenshot:

The snapshot file now contains the React tree of our `AddCar` component. You can see part of the snapshot file from the beginning in the following code block:

```
// Jest Snapshot v1, https://goo.gl/fbAQLP

exports[`renders a snapshot 1`] = `
<div>
  <button
    className="MuiButtonBase-root-252 MuiButton-root-226 MuiButton-
outlined-234
      MuiButton-outlinedPrimary-235"
    disabled={false}
    onBlur={[Function]}
    onClick={[Function]}
    onContextMenu={[Function]}
    onFocus={[Function]}
    onKeyDown={[Function]}
    onKeyUp={[Function]}
    onMouseDown={[Function]}
    onMouseLeave={[Function]}
    onMouseUp={[Function]}
    onTouchEnd={[Function]}
    onTouchMove={[Function]}
    onTouchStart={[Function]}
    style={
      Object {
        "margin": 10,
      }
    }
    tabIndex="0"
    type="button"
  >
  ...continue
```

Now, let's look at how we can use Enzyme to test our React components.

Using Enzyme

Enzyme is a JavaScript library for testing React components' output, and was developed by Airbnb. Enzyme has a really nice API for DOM manipulation and traversing. If you have used jQuery, it is really easy to understand the idea of the Enzyme API.

To start using Enzyme, perform the following steps:

1. Install it by typing the following command in your Terminal. This will install the enzyme library and the adapter library for React version 16. There is an adapter available for older React versions:

   ```
   npm install enzyme enzyme-adapter-react-16 --save-dev
   ```

2. Create a new test file (test suite) called AddCar.test.js in the src folder. Now, we are going to create an Enzyme shallow rendering test for our AddCar component. The first test case renders the component and checks that there are five TextInput components, as there should be. wrapper.find finds every node in the render tree that matches TextInput. With Enzyme tests, we can use Jest for assertions, and here, we are using toHaveLength to check that the established node count equals five. Shallow rendering tests the component as a unit and does not render any child components. For this case, shallow rendering is enough. Otherwise, you can also use the full DOM rendering by using mount:

   ```
   import React from 'react';
   import AddCar from './components/AddCar';
   import Enzyme, { shallow } from 'enzyme';
   import Adapter from 'enzyme-adapter-react-16';

   Enzyme.configure({ adapter: new Adapter() });

   describe('<AddCar />', () => {
     it('renders five <TextInput /> components', () => {
       const wrapper = shallow(<AddCar />);
       expect(wrapper.find('TextField')).toHaveLength(5);
     });
   });
   ```

3. Now, if you run the tests, you can see the following message in the Terminal. You can also see that the number of test suites is two, because the new test file and all tests passed:

   ```
   PASS  src\AddCar.test.js

   Test Suites: 2 passed, 2 total
   Tests:       3 passed, 3 total
   Snapshots:   1 passed, 1 total
   Time:        6.212s
   Ran all test suites.
   ```

We have now learned the basics of frontend testing. Next, we will learn how to secure our app.

Summary

In this chapter, we provided a basic overview of how to test React apps. Jest is a testing library developed by Facebook, and it is already available in our frontend because we created our app with `create-react-app`.

We created a couple of tests with Jest and ran those tests to see how you can check the results of tests. We installed Enzyme, which is a test utility for React. With Enzyme, you can easily test your React component rendering and events.

In the next chapter, we will secure our application, and add the login functionality to the frontend.

Questions

1. What is Jest?
2. How should you create test cases using Jest?
3. How should you create a snapshot test using Jest?
4. What is Enzyme?
5. How should you install Enzyme?
6. How should you test rendering with Enzyme?

Further reading

Packt has other great resources available for learning about React and testing. These are as follows:

- *React 16 Tooling*, by Adam Boduch (https://www.packtpub.com/web-development/react-16-tooling)
- *Jasmine JavaScript Testing – Second Edition*, by Paulo Ragonha (https://www.packtpub.com/web-development/jasmine-javascript-testing-second-edition)

Securing Your Application 14

This chapter will explain how to implement authentication to our frontend when we are using JWT authentication in the backend. At the beginning, we will switch on security in our backend to enable JWT authentication. Then, we will create a component for the login functionality. Finally, we will modify our CRUD functionalities to send the token in the request's `Authorization` header to the backend.

In this chapter, we will cover the following topics:

- Securing the backend
- Securing the frontend

Technical requirements

The Spring Boot application that we created in Chapter 5, *Securing and Testing Your Backend*, is required (is located on GitHub at: `https://github.com/PacktPublishing/Hands-On-Full-Stack-Development-with-Spring-Boot-2-and-React-Second-Edition/tree/master/Chapter05`), as is the React app that we used in Chapter 12, *Styling the Frontend with React Material-UI* (is located on GitHub at: `https://github.com/PacktPublishing/Hands-On-Full-Stack-Development-with-Spring-Boot-2-and-React-Second-Edition/tree/master/Chapter12`).

The following GitHub link will also be required: `https://github.com/PacktPublishing/Hands-On-Full-Stack-Development-with-Spring-Boot-2-and-React-Second-Edition/tree/master/Chapter14`.

Securing the backend

We have implemented CRUD functionalities in our frontend using an unsecured backend. Now, it is time to switch on security for our backend and go back to the version that we created in Chapter 5, *Securing and Testing Your Backend*:

1. Open your backend project with the Eclipse IDE and open the SecurityConfig.java file in the editor view. We have commented the security out and have allowed everyone access to all endpoints. Now, we can remove that line and also remove the comments from the original version. Now, your SecurityConfig.java file's configure method should look like the following:

```
@Override
  protected void configure(HttpSecurity http) throws Exception {
    http.csrf().disable().cors().and().authorizeRequests()
    .antMatchers(HttpMethod.POST, "/login").permitAll()
    .anyRequest().authenticated()
    .and()
    // Filter for the api/login requests
    .addFilterBefore(new LoginFilter("/login",
authenticationManager()),
        UsernamePasswordAuthenticationFilter.class)
    // Filter for other requests to check JWT in header
    .addFilterBefore(new AuthenticationFilter(),
        UsernamePasswordAuthenticationFilter.class);
}
```

Let's test what happens when the backend is secured again.

2. Run the backend by pressing the **Run** button in Eclipse and check from the **Console** view that the application started correctly. Run the frontend by typing the npm start command into your Terminal, and the browser should be opened to the address localhost:3000.

3. You should now see that the list page and the table are empty. If you open the developer tools, you will notice that the request ends in a 403 Forbidden HTTP error. This is actually what we wanted, because we haven't yet executed authentication in relation to our frontend:

Now, we are ready to work with the frontend.

Securing the frontend

The authentication was implemented to the backend using JWT. In `Chapter 5`, *Securing and Testing Your Backend*, we created JWT authentication, and the `/login` endpoint is allowed to everyone without authentication. In the frontend's login page, we have to first call the `/login` endpoint to get the token. After that, the token will be included in all requests we are sending to the backend, as demonstrated in `Chapter 5`, *Securing and Testing Your Backend*.

Let's first create a login component that asks for credentials from the user to get a token from the backend:

1. Create a new file, called `Login.js`, in the `components` folder. Now, the file structure of the frontend should be the following:

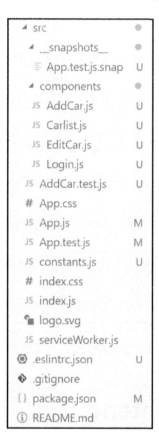

2. Open the file in the VS Code editor view and add the following base code to the login component. We are also importing `SERVER_URL`, because it is required in a login request:

```
import React, { useState } from 'react';
import {SERVER_URL} from '../constants.js';

const Login = () => {
  return (
    <div>
    </div>
```

```
    );
  }

  export default Login;
```

3. We need three state values for the authentication, two for the credentials (`username` and `password`), and one Boolean value to indicate the status of the authentication. The default value of the authentication status state is `false`. We introduce states using the `useState` function:

```
const [user, setUser] = useState({username: '', password: ''})
const [isAuthenticated, setAuth] = useState(false);
```

4. In the user interface, we are going to use the Material-UI component library, as we did with the rest of the user interface. We need text field components for the credentials and a button to call a login function. Add imports for the components to the `login.js` file:

```
import TextField from '@material-ui/core/TextField';
import Button from '@material-ui/core/Button';
```

5. Add imported components to a user interface by adding these to the `return` statement. We need two `TextField` components, one for the username and one for the password. One `Button` component is needed to call the `login` function that we are going to implement later in this section:

```
return (
  <div>
    <TextField name="username"
      label="Username" onChange={handleChange} /><br/>
    <TextField type="password" name="password"
      label="Password" onChange={handleChange} /><br/><br/>
    <Button variant="outlined" color="primary"
      onClick={login}>
      Login
    </Button>
  </div>
);
```

6. Implement the change handler for the `TextField` components, in order to save typed values to the states:

```
const handleChange = (event) => {
  setUser({...user, [event.target.name] : event.target.value})
}
```

7. As shown in Chapter 5, *Securing and Testing Your Backend*, the login is done by calling the /login endpoint using the POST method and sending the user object inside the body. If authentication succeeds, we get a token in a response Authorization header. We will then save the token to session storage and set the isAuthenticated state value to true. The session storage is similar to local storage, but it is cleared when a page session ends. When the isAuthenticated state value is changed, the user interface is rerendered:

```
const login = () => {
  fetch(SERVER_URL + 'login', {
    method: 'POST',
    body: JSON.stringify(user)
  })
  .then(res => {
    const jwtToken = res.headers.get('Authorization');
    if (jwtToken !== null) {
      sessionStorage.setItem("jwt", jwtToken);
      setAuth(true);
    }
  })
  .catch(err => console.error(err))
}
```

8. We can implement conditional rendering, which renders the Login component if the isAuthenticated state is false, or the Carlist component if the isAuthenticated state is true. We first have to import the Carlist component to the Login component:

```
import Carlist from './Carlist';
```

Then, we have to implement the following changes to the return statement:

```
if (isAuthenticated === true) {
  return (<Carlist />)
}
else {
  return (
    <div>
      <TextField name="username"
        label="Username" onChange={handleChange} /><br/>
      <TextField type="password" name="password"
        label="Password" onChange={handleChange} /><br/><br/>
      <Button variant="outlined" color="primary"
        onClick={login}>
        Login
      </Button>
```

```
      </div>
    );
  }
```

9. To show the login form, we have to render the Login component instead of the Carlist component in the App.js file:

```
// App.js
import React from 'react';
import './App.css';
import AppBar from '@material-ui/core/AppBar';
import Toolbar from '@material-ui/core/Toolbar';
import Typography from '@material-ui/core/Typography';
import Login from './components/Login';

function App() {
 return (
 <div className="App">
 <AppBar position="static" color="default">
 <Toolbar>
 <Typography variant="h6" color="inherit">
 CarList
 </Typography>
 </Toolbar>
 </AppBar>
 <Login />
 </div>
 );
}

export default App;
```

Now, when your frontend and backend are running, your frontend should look like the following screenshot:

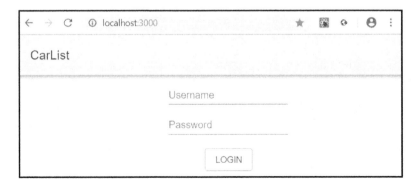

If you log in using the user/user or admin/admin credentials, you should see the **CarList** page. If you open the developer tools, you can see that the token is now saved to session storage:

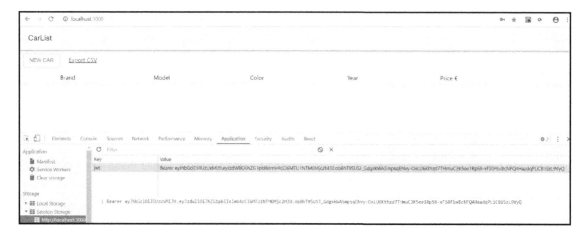

The car list is still empty, but that is correct, because we haven't included the token to the request yet. That is required for JWT authentication, which we will implement in the next phase:

1. Open the Carlist.js file in the VS Code editor view. To fetch the cars, we first have to read the token from the session storage and then add the Authorization header with the token value to the request. You can see the source code of the fetch function here:

```
// Carlist.js
// Fetch all cars
fetchCars = () => {
  // Read the token from the session storage
  // and include it to Authorization header
  const token = sessionStorage.getItem("jwt");
  fetch(SERVER_URL + 'api/cars',
  {
    headers: {'Authorization': token}
  })
  .then((response) => response.json())
  .then((responseData) => {
    this.setState({
      cars: responseData._embedded.cars,
    });
  })
```

```
        .catch(err => console.error(err));
    }
```

2. If you log in to your frontend, you should see the car list populated with cars from the database:

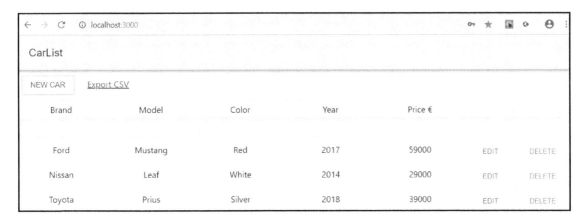

3. Check the request content from the developer tools; you can see that it contains the `Authorization` header with the token value:

All other CRUD functionalities require the same modification to work correctly. The source code of the `delete` function appears as follows, after the modifications:

```
// Delete car
onDelClick = (link) => {
  if (window.confirm('Are you sure to delete?')) {
    const token = sessionStorage.getItem("jwt");
    fetch(link,
    {
      method: 'DELETE',
      headers: {'Authorization': token}
    })
    .then(res => {
      toast.success("Car deleted", {
        position: toast.POSITION.BOTTOM_LEFT
      });
      this.fetchCars();
    })
    .catch(err => {
      toast.error("Error when deleting", {
        position: toast.POSITION.BOTTOM_LEFT
      });
      console.error(err)
    })
  }
}
```

The source code of the `add` function appears as follows, after the modifications:

```
// Add new car
addCar(car) {
  const token = sessionStorage.getItem("jwt");
  fetch(SERVER_URL + 'api/cars',
  { method: 'POST',
    headers: {
      'Content-Type': 'application/json',
      'Authorization': token
    },
    body: JSON.stringify(car)
  })
  .then(res => this.fetchCars())
  .catch(err => console.error(err))
}
```

Finally, the source code of the `update` function looks like this:

```
// Update car
updateCar(car, link) {
  const token = sessionStorage.getItem("jwt");
  fetch(link,
  { method: 'PUT',
    headers: {
      'Content-Type': 'application/json',
      'Authorization': token
    },
    body: JSON.stringify(car)
  })
  .then(res => {
    toast.success("Changes saved", {
      position: toast.POSITION.BOTTOM_LEFT
    });
    this.fetchCars();
  })
  .catch(err =>
    toast.error("Error when saving", {
      position: toast.POSITION.BOTTOM_LEFT
    })
  )
}
```

Now, all the CRUD functionalities will be working after you have logged in to the application.

In the final phase, we are going to implement an error message that is shown to an end user if authentication fails. We are using the `react-toastify` component to show the message:

1. Add the following import to the `Login.js` file:

```
import { ToastContainer, toast } from 'react-toastify';
import 'react-toastify/dist/ReactToastify.css';
```

2. Add `ToastContainer` to the `render()` method:

```
<ToastContainer autoClose={1500} />
```

3. Show the `toast` message if authentication fails:

```
const login = () => {
  fetch(SERVER_URL + 'login', {
    method: 'POST',
    body: JSON.stringify(user)
  })
```

```
    .then(res => {
      const jwtToken = res.headers.get('Authorization');
      if (jwtToken !== null) {
        sessionStorage.setItem("jwt", jwtToken);
        setAuth(true);
      }
      else {
        toast.warn("Check your username and password", {
          position: toast.POSITION.BOTTOM_LEFT
        })
      }
    })
    .catch(err => console.error(err))
}
```

If you now log in with the wrong credentials, you will see the `toast` message:

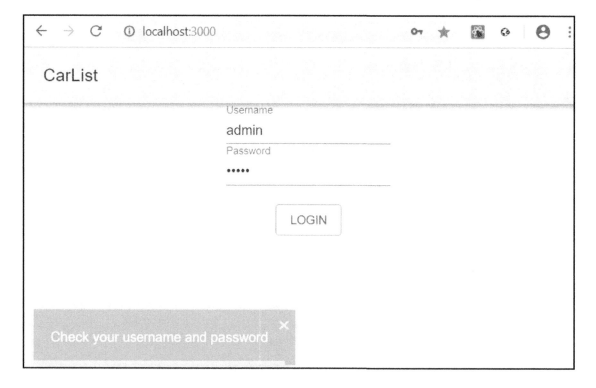

The logout functionality is much more straightforward to implement. You basically just have to remove the token from session storage and change the `isAuthenticated` state value to `false`, as shown in the following source code:

```
const logout = () => {
  sessionStorage.removeItem("jwt");
  setAuth(false);
}
```

Then, with conditional rendering, you can render the `Login` component instead of `Carlist`.

If you want to implement a menu using React Router, it is possible to implement so-called secured routes that can be accessed only when a user is authenticated. The following source code shows the secured route that presents the routed component if the user is authenticated; otherwise, it redirects to a login page:

```
const SecuredRoute = ({ component: Component, ...rest, isAuthenticated })
=> (
  <Route {...rest} render={props => (
    isAuthenticated ? (
      <Component {...props}/>
    ) : (
      <Redirect to={{
        pathname: '/login',
        state: { from: props.location }
      }}/>
    )
  )}/>
)
```

Here is an example of a `Switch` router that is using `SecuredRoute`, which we defined in the previous example:

```
<Switch>
  <Route path="/login" component={Login} />
  <Route path="/contact" component={Contact} />
  <SecuredRoute isAuthenticated={this.state.isAuthenticated}
    path="/shop" component={Shop} />
  <Route render={() => <h1>Page not found</h1>} />
</Switch>
```

Now, the `Login` and `Contact` components can be accessed without authentication, but `Shop` requires authentication.

Summary

In this chapter, you learned how to implement a login functionality for our frontend when you are using JWT authentication. Following successful authentication, we used session storage to save the token that we received from the backend. The token was then used in all requests that we sent to the backend. Therefore, we had to modify our CRUD functionalities to work with authentication properly.

In the next chapter, we will deploy our application to Heroku, as we demonstrate how to create Docker containers.

Questions

1. How should you create a login form?
2. How should you log in to the backend using JWT?
3. How should you store tokens in session storage?
4. How should you send a token to the backend in CRUD functions?

Further reading

Packt has other great resources available for learning about React. These are as follows:

- *React 16 Tooling*, by Adam Boduch (https://www.packtpub.com/web-development/react-16-tooling)
- *React 16 Essentials – Second Edition*, by Adam Boduch and Artemij Fedosejev (https://www.packtpub.com/web-development/react-16-essentials-second-edition)

15
Deploying Your Application

This chapter will explain how to deploy your backend and frontend to a server. There's a variety of cloud servers, or **PaaS** (short for **Platform as a Service**) providers, available, such as **Amazon Web Services (AWS)**, DigitalOcean, and Microsoft Azure. In this book, we are using Heroku, which supports multiple programming languages that are used in web development. We will also show you how to use Docker containers in deployment.

In this chapter, we will cover the following topics:

- Different options for deploying the Spring Boot application
- How to deploy the Spring Boot application to Heroku
- How to deploy the React app to Heroku
- How to create the Spring Boot and MariaDB Docker container

Technical requirements

The Spring Boot application that we created in Chapter 5, *Securing and Testing Your Backend*, is required (it is available on GitHub at: https://github.com/PacktPublishing/ Hands-On-Full-Stack-Development-with-Spring-Boot-2-and-React-Second-Edition/ tree/master/Chapter05), as is the React app that we used in Chapter 13, *Testing Your Frontend* (it is available on GitHub at: https://github.com/PacktPublishing/Hands-On- Full-Stack-Development-with-Spring-Boot-2-and-React-Second-Edition/tree/master/ Chapter13).

Docker installation is necessary, and the following GitHub link will also be required: https://github.com/PacktPublishing/Hands-On-Full-Stack-Development- with-Spring-Boot-2-and-React-Second-Edition/tree/master/Chapter15.

Deploying the backend

If you are going to use your own server, the easiest way to deploy the Spring Boot application is to use an executable JAR file. If you use Maven, an executable JAR file is generated by typing the `mvn clean install` command in the command line. That command creates the JAR file in the `build` folder. In this case, you don't have to install a separate application server, because it is embedded in your JAR file. Then, you just have to run the JAR file using the `java` command, `java -jar your_appfile.jar`. The embedded Tomcat version can be defined in the `pom.xml` file, with the following lines:

```
<properties>
  <tomcat.version>8.0.52</tomcat.version>
</properties>
```

If you are using a separate application server, you have to create a WAR package. This is slightly more complicated, and you have to make some modifications to your application. The following are the steps that have to be observed in order to create the WAR file:

1. Modify an application's `main` class by extending `SpringBootServletIntializer` and overriding the `configure` method:

    ```
    @SpringBootApplication
    public class Application extends SpringBootServletInitializer {
        @Override
        protected SpringApplicationBuilder configure
            (SpringApplicationBuilder application) {
            return application.sources(Application.class);
        }

        public static void main(String[] args) throws Exception {
            SpringApplication.run(Application.class, args);
        }
    }
    ```

2. Change the packaging from JAR to WAR in the `pom.xml` file:

    ```
    <packaging>war</packaging>
    ```

3. Add the following dependency to the `pom.xml` file. Then, the Tomcat application is no longer embedded:

```
<dependency>
  <groupId>org.springframework.boot</groupId>
  <artifactId>spring-boot-starter-tomcat</artifactId>
  <scope>provided</scope>
</dependency>
```

Now, when you build your application, the WAR file is generated. It can be deployed to the existing Tomcat by copying the file to Tomcat's `/webapps` folder.

Nowadays, cloud servers are the principal means of providing your application to end users. Next, we are going to deploy our backend to the Heroku cloud server (`https://www. heroku.com/`). Heroku offers a free account that you can use to deploy your own applications. With the free account, your applications go to sleep after 30 minutes of inactivity, and it takes a little bit more time to restart the application. However, the free account is sufficient for testing and hobby purposes.

For deployment, you can use Heroku's web-based user interface. The following steps will take you through the deployment process:

1. After you have created an account with Heroku, log in to the Heroku website. Navigate to the dashboard that shows a list of your applications. There is a button called **New** that opens a menu. Select **Create new app** from the menu:

2. Name your app, select a region, and press the **Create app** button:

3. Select a deployment method. There are several options; we are using the **GitHub** option. In this method, you first have to push your application to GitHub, and then link your GitHub repository to Heroku:

4. Search for a repository you want to deploy to, and then press the **Connect** button:

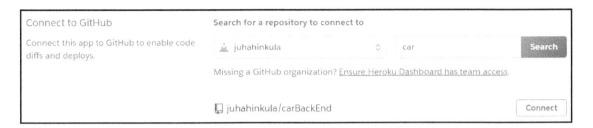

5. Choose between an automatic and manual deployment. The automatic option deploys your app automatically when you push a new version to connect to the GitHub repository. You also have to select a branch you want to deploy. We will use the manual option that deploys the app when you press the **Deploy branch** button:

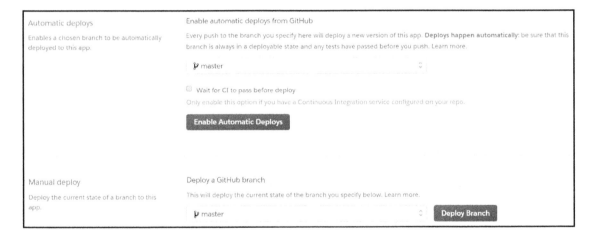

6. Deployment starts, and you can see a build log. You should see a message that says **Your app was successfully deployed**:

Now, your application is deployed to the Heroku cloud server. If you are using the H2 in-memory database, this will be enough, and your application should work. We are using MariaDB. Therefore, we have to install the database.

In Heroku, we can use `JawsDB`, which is available in Heroku as an add-on. JawsDB is a **Database as a Service (DBaaS)** provider that offers the MariaDB database, which can be used in Heroku. The following steps describe how to start using the database:

1. Open a **Resources** tab in your Heroku app page and type `JawsDB` into the **Add-ons** search field:

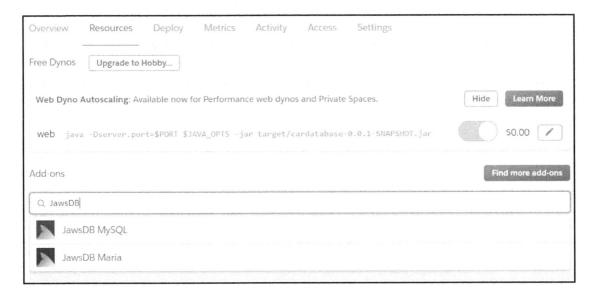

2. Select **JawsDB Maria** from the drop-down list. Click on **JawsDB**, and you will see the connection information of your database:

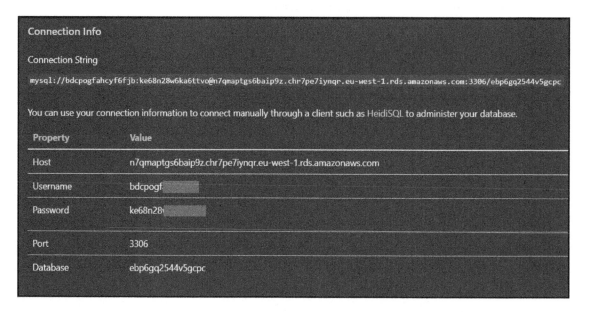

3. Change the database connection definition in the `application.properties` file with the values from the JawsDB **Connection Info** page. In this example, we use a plain password, but it is recommended that you encrypt a password using, for example, the **Java Simplified Encryption (JASYPT)** library:

```
spring.datasource.url=jdbc:mariadb://n7qmaptgs6baip9z.chr7pe7iynqr.
eu-west-1.rds.amazonaws.com:3306/ebp6gq2544v5gcpc
spring.datasource.username=bdcpogfxxxxxxx
spring.datasource.password=ke68n28xxxxxxx
spring.datasource.driver-class-name=org.mariadb.jdbc.Driver
```

4. With the free account, we can have a maximum of 10 concurrent connections to our database; therefore, we also have to add the following line to the `application.properties` file:

```
spring.datasource.max-active=10
```

5. Push your changes to GitHub and deploy your app in Heroku. Now, your application is ready, and you can test that with Postman. The URL of the app is `https://carbackend.herokuapp.com/`, but you can also use your own domain. If we send the `POST` request to the `/login` endpoint with the credential, we can get the token in the response header. So, everything seems to work properly:

We can also connect to the JawsDB database with HeidiSQL, and we can see that our **car** database has been created:

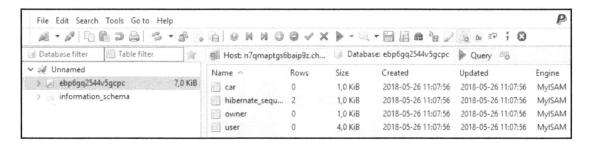

We can watch application logs by selecting **View logs** from the **More** menu:

The application log view looks like the following:

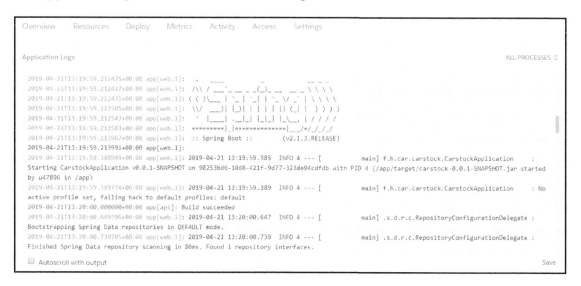

Now, we are ready to deploy our frontend.

Deploying the frontend

In this section, we will deploy our React frontend to Heroku. The easiest way to deploy the React app to Heroku is to use the Heroku Buildpack for `create-react-app` (`https://github.com/mars/create-react-app-buildpack`). For deployment, we have to install the Heroku CLI, which is the command-line tool for Heroku. You can download the installation package from `https://devcenter.heroku.com/articles/heroku-cli`. Once installation is complete, you can use the Heroku CLI from PowerShell or the Terminal you're using. The following steps describe the deployment process:

1. Open your frontend project with VS Code and open the `constant.js` file in the editor. Change the `SERVER_URL` constant to match our backend's URL, and save the changes:

   ```
   export const SERVER_URL = 'https://carbackend.herokuapp.com/'
   ```

2. Create a local Git repository for your project and commit the files, if you haven't done that yet. Navigate to your project folder with the Git command-line tool and type the following commands:

   ```
   git init
   git add .
   git commit -m "Heroku deployment"
   ```

3. The following command creates a new Heroku app and asks for credentials to log in to Heroku. Replace `[APPNAME]` with your own app name. Once the command has been executed, you should see the new app in your Heroku dashboard:

   ```
   heroku create [APPNAME] --buildpack
   https://github.com/mars/create-react-app-buildpack.git
   ```

4. Deploy your code to Heroku by typing the following command in PowerShell:

   ```
   git push heroku master
   ```

Once the deployment is ready, you should see the `Verifying deploy... done` message in PowerShell, as shown in the following screenshot:

```
remote:
remote: The build folder is ready to be deployed.
remote: You may serve it with a static server:
remote:
remote:   yarn global add serve
remote:   serve -s build
remote:
remote: Find out more about deployment here:
remote:
remote:   http://bit.ly/2vY88Kr
remote:
remote: =====> Downloading Buildpack: https://github.com/heroku/heroku-buildpack-static.git
remote: =====> Detected Framework: Static HTML
remote:    % Total    % Received % Xferd  Average Speed   Time    Time     Time  Current
remote:                                   Dload  Upload   Total   Spent    Left  Speed
remote: 100  838k  100  838k    0     0  5894k      0 --:--:-- --:--:-- --:--:-- 5905k
remote: -----> Installed directory to /app/bin
remote: Using release configuration from last framework (Static HTML).
remote: -----> Discovering process types
remote:        Procfile declares types    -> (none)
remote:        Default types for buildpack -> web
remote:
remote: -----> Compressing...
remote:        Done: 47.6M
remote: -----> Launching...
remote:        Released v4
remote:        https://carfront.herokuapp.com/ deployed to Heroku
remote:
remote: Verifying deploy... done.
To https://git.heroku.com/carfront.git
   32a5ecd..4565486  master -> master
```

Now, you can go to your Heroku dashboard and see the URL of your frontend; you can also open it from the Heroku CLI by typing the `heroku open` command. If you navigate to your frontend, you should see the login form, as follows:

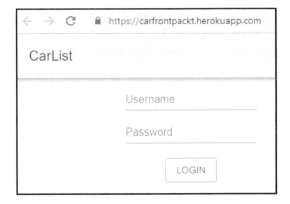

In the next section, you will learn how to use Docker containers.

Using Docker containers

Docker is a container platform that makes software development, deployment, and shipping easier. Containers are lightweight and executable software packages that include everything that is needed to run software. In this section, we are creating a container from our Spring Boot backend, as follows:

1. Install Docker on your workstation. You can find the installation packages at `https://www.docker.com/get-docker`. There are installation packages for multiple platforms, and if you have a Windows operating system, you can go through the installation wizard using the default settings.
2. The Spring Boot application is just an executable JAR file that can be executed with Java. The JAR file can be created with the following Maven command:

   ```
   mvn clean install
   ```

You can also use Eclipse to run Maven goals by opening the **Run | Run configurations...** menu. Select your project in the **Base directory** field, using the **Workspace** button. Type **clean install** into the **Goals** field and press the **Run** button:

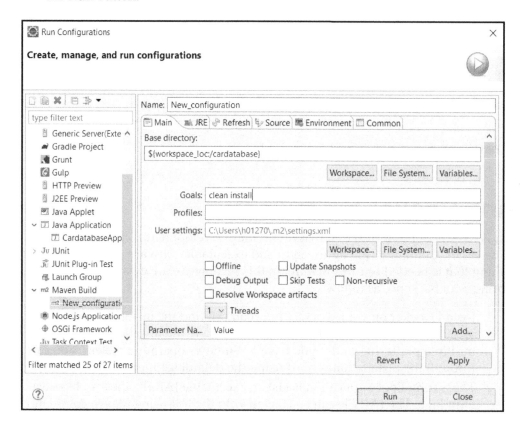

3. Once the build is finished, you can find the executable JAR file from the /target folder:

4. You can test that the build has executed correctly by running the JAR file with the following command:

```
java -jar .\cardatabase-0.0.1-SNAPSHOT.jar
```

5. You'll see the application's starting messages, and finally, your application will be running:

```
  .   ____          _            __ _ _
 /\\ / ___'_ __ _ _(_)_ __  __ _ \ \ \ \
( ( )\___ | '_ | '_| | '_ \/ _` | \ \ \ \
 \\/  ___)| |_)| | | | | || (_| |  ) ) ) )
  '  |____| .__|_| |_|_| |_\__, | / / / /
 =========|_|==============|___/=/_/_/_/
 :: Spring Boot ::        (v2.1.3.RELEASE)

2019-04-21 16:35:21.017  INFO 61816 --- [           main] c.p.cardatabase.CardatabaseApplication   : Starting Cardatab
aseApplication v0.0.1-SNAPSHOT on HHMX4717 with PID 61816 (C:\work\Chapter05\target\cardatabase-0.0.1-SNAPSHOT.jar sta
rted by h01270 in C:\work\Chapter05\target)
2019-04-21 16:35:21.020  INFO 61816 --- [           main] c.p.cardatabase.CardatabaseApplication   : No active profile
 set, falling back to default profiles: default
2019-04-21 16:35:22.191  INFO 61816 --- [           main] .s.d.r.c.RepositoryConfigurationDelegate : Bootstrapping Spr
ing Data repositories in DEFAULT mode.
2019-04-21 16:35:22.274  INFO 61816 --- [           main] .s.d.r.c.RepositoryConfigurationDelegate : Finished Spring D
ata repository scanning in 73ms. Found 3 repository interfaces.
2019-04-21 16:35:22.805  INFO 61816 --- [           main] trationDelegate$BeanPostProcessorChecker : Bean 'org.springf
ramework.transaction.annotation.ProxyTransactionManagementConfiguration' of type [org.springframework.transaction.anno
tation.ProxyTransactionManagementConfiguration$$EnhancerBySpringCGLIB$$f198b871] is not eligible for getting processed
 by all BeanPostProcessors (for example: not eligible for auto-proxying)
2019-04-21 16:35:22.839  INFO 61816 --- [           main] trationDelegate$BeanPostProcessorChecker : Bean 'org.springf
ramework.hateoas.config.HateoasConfiguration' of type [org.springframework.hateoas.config.HateoasConfiguration$$Enhanc
erBySpringCGLIB$$711905a3] is not eligible for getting processed by all BeanPostProcessors (for example: not eligible
for auto-proxying)
2019-04-21 16:35:23.775  INFO 61816 --- [           main] o.s.b.w.embedded.tomcat.TomcatWebServer  : Tomcat initialize
d with port(s): 8080 (http)
2019-04-21 16:35:23.816  INFO 61816 --- [           main] o.apache.catalina.core.StandardService   : Starting service
[Tomcat]
2019-04-21 16:35:23.816  INFO 61816 --- [           main] org.apache.catalina.core.StandardEngine  : Starting Servlet
engine: [Apache Tomcat/9.0.16]
```

Containers are defined by using Dockerfiles.

6. Create a new `Dockerfile` in the root folder of your project and name it `Dockerfile`. The following lines show the contents of the `Dockerfile`. We are using Alpine Linux. `EXPOSE` defines the port that should be published outside of the container. `COPY` copies the JAR file to the container's filesystem and renames it `app.jar`. `ENTRYPOINT` defines the command-line arguments that the Docker container runs.

There is also a Maven plugin available to build Docker images. It is developed by Spotify and can be found at `https://github.com/spotify/docker-maven-plugin`.

The following lines show the contents of `Dockerfile`:

```
FROM openjdk:8-jdk-alpine
VOLUME /tmp
EXPOSE 8080
ARG JAR_FILE
COPY target/cardatabase-0.0.1-SNAPSHOT.jar app.jar
ENTRYPOINT ["java","-Djava.security.egd=file:/dev/./urandom","-
jar","/app.jar"]
```

7. Create the container with the following command. With the `-t` argument, we can give a friendly name to our container:

   `docker build -t carbackend .`

   At the end of the `build` command, you should see the **Successfully built** message:

```
PS C:\work\carBackEnd> docker build -t carbackend .
Sending build context to Docker daemon  32.67MB
Step 1/5 : FROM openjdk:8-jdk-alpine
 ---> 224765a6bdbe
Step 2/5 : VOLUME /tmp
 ---> Using cache
 ---> a03de6ca0e4e
Step 3/5 : ARG JAR_FILE
 ---> Using cache
 ---> f237684c815f
Step 4/5 : COPY target/cardatabase-0.0.1-SNAPSHOT.jar app.jar
 ---> Using cache
 ---> 13c0ee6b4cd2
Step 5/5 : ENTRYPOINT ["java","-Djava.security.egd=file:/dev/./urandom","-jar","/app.jar"]
 ---> Using cache
 ---> 7edc33ec6be6
Successfully built 7edc33ec6be6
Successfully tagged carbackend:latest
```

8. Check the list of the container using the `docker image ls` command:

```
PS C:\work\carBackEnd> docker image ls
REPOSITORY          TAG              IMAGE ID          CREATED            SIZE
carbackend          latest           7edc33ec6be6      2 minutes ago      134MB
openjdk             8-jdk-alpine     224765a6bdbe      4 months ago       102MB
```

9. Run the container with the following command:

```
docker run -p 4000:8080 carbackend
```

The Spring Boot application starts, but it ends with an error, because we are trying to access the localhost database. The localhost now points to the container itself, and there is no MariaDB installed.

10. We will create our own container for MariaDB. You can pull the latest MariaDB container from the Docker Hub using the following command:

```
docker pull mariadb:lates
```

11. Run the MariaDB container. The following command sets the root user password and creates a new database, called `cardb`, that we need for our Spring Boot application:

```
docker run --name cardb -e MYSQL_ROOT_PASSWORD=pwd -e
MYSQL_DATABASE=cardb mariadb
```

12. We have to make one change to our Spring Boot `application.properties` file. Change the `datasource` URL to the following. In the next step, we will specify that our application can access the database container using the `mariadb` name. Once this change has been made, you have to build your application and recreate the Spring Boot container:

```
spring.datasource.url=jdbc:mariadb://mariadb:3306/cardb
```

13. We can run our Spring Boot container and link the MariaDB container to it using the following command. This command now stipulates that our Spring Boot container can access the MariaDB container using the `mariadb` name:

```
docker run -p 8080:8080 --name carapp --link cardb:mariadb -d
carbackend
```

14. We can also access our application logs by typing the `docker logs carapp` command:

```
s): 8080 (http) with context path ''
2018-05-27 12:48:34.234  INFO 1 --- [          main] c.p.cardatabase.CardatabaseApplication   : Started CardatabaseAppl
ication in 6.67 seconds (JVM running for 7.3)
Hibernate: select next_val as id_val from hibernate_sequence for update
Hibernate: update hibernate_sequence set next_val= ? where next_val=?
Hibernate: insert into owner (firstname, lastname, ownerid) values (?, ?, ?)
Hibernate: select next_val as id_val from hibernate_sequence for update
Hibernate: update hibernate_sequence set next_val= ? where next_val=?
Hibernate: insert into owner (firstname, lastname, ownerid) values (?, ?, ?)
Hibernate: select next_val as id_val from hibernate_sequence for update
Hibernate: update hibernate_sequence set next_val= ? where next_val=?
Hibernate: insert into car (brand, color, model, owner, price, register_number, year, id) values (?, ?, ?, ?, ?, ?, ?, ?, ?
)
Hibernate: select next_val as id_val from hibernate_sequence for update
Hibernate: update hibernate_sequence set next_val= ? where next_val=?
Hibernate: insert into car (brand, color, model, owner, price, register_number, year, id) values (?, ?, ?, ?, ?, ?, ?, ?
)
Hibernate: select next_val as id_val from hibernate_sequence for update
Hibernate: update hibernate_sequence set next_val= ? where next_val=?
Hibernate: insert into car (brand, color, model, owner, price, register_number, year, id) values (?, ?, ?, ?, ?, ?, ?, ?
)
Hibernate: insert into user (password, role, username) values (?, ?, ?)
Hibernate: insert into user (password, role, username) values (?, ?, ?)
```

We can see that our application has started successfully, and the demo data has been inserted into the database that exists in the MariaDB container.

Summary

In this chapter, you learned how to deploy the Spring Boot application. We went through the different deployment options for the Spring Boot application and deployed the application to Heroku. Next, we deployed our React frontend to Heroku using the Heroku Buildpack for `create-react-app`, which makes the deployment process faster. Finally, we used Docker to create containers from our Spring Boot application and the MariaDB database.

In the next chapter, we will cover some more technologies and best practices that you should explore.

Questions

1. How should you create a Spring Boot executable JAR file?
2. How should you deploy the Spring Boot application to Heroku?
3. How should you deploy the React app to Heroku?
4. What is Docker?
5. How should you create the Spring Boot application container?
6. How should you create the MariaDB container?

Further reading

Packt has other great resources available for learning about React, Spring Boot, and Docker. These are as follows:

- *React 16 Tooling*, by Adam Boduch (https://www.packtpub.com/web-development/react-16-tooling)
- *React 16 Essentials – Second Edition*, by Adam Boduch and Artemij Fedosejev (https://www.packtpub.com/web-development/react-16-essentials-second-edition)
- *Deployment with Docker*, by Srdjan Grubor (https://www.packtpub.com/virtualization-and-cloud/deployment-docker)
- *Docker Fundamentals*, by Sreeprakash Neelakantan (https://www.packtpub.com/virtualization-and-cloud/docker-fundamentals-integrated-course)

16
Best Practices

This chapter will go through some points that you should know if you want to become a full stack developer, or if you want to progress further in your software development career. We will also go over some best practices that are worth keeping in mind when you're working in the field of software development.

In this chapter, we will cover the following topics:

- What kind of technologies you should know
- What kinds of best practices are important to you?

What to learn next

To become a full stack developer, you have to be able to work with both the backend and the frontend. That sounds like quite a challenging task, but if you focus on the right things and don't try to master everything, it is possible. Nowadays, the technology stack available is huge, and you might often wonder what you should learn next. There are multiple factors that may give you a few hints about where to go next. One way to find out is to browse job opportunities and see which technologies companies are looking for.

There are multiple approaches, and no single right path, when it comes to setting out on learning a new technology. The use of programming web courses is a really popular starting point and it gives you the basic knowledge to start the learning process. The process is never-ending, because technologies are developing and changing all the time.

An understanding of the following technologies is necessary if you want to become a full stack developer. This is not a complete list, but it is a good starting point.

HTML

HTML is the most fundamental thing that you should learn in web development. You don't have to master all the details of HTML, but you should have a good basic knowledge of it. HTML 5 introduced a lot of new features that are also worth learning.

CSS

CSS is also a very basic thing to learn. One good aspect is the fact that there are lots of good tutorials available for both HTML and CSS. It is a good idea to learn about the use of some CSS libraries, such as Bootstrap, which is widely used. CSS preprocessors, such as SASS and LESS, are also worth learning.

HTTP

The HTTP protocol is key when developing web applications and RESTful web services. You have to understand the basics of HTTP and know its limitations. You should also know what kinds of methods exist, and how to use these with different programming languages.

JavaScript

JavaScript is definitely a programming language that you should master. Without JavaScript skills, it is really hard to work with modern frontend development. ES6 is also good to learn, because that makes JavaScript coding cleaner and more efficient.

A backend programming language

It's hard to survive without knowing a few programming languages. If JavaScript is used for frontend development, it can also be used in the backend with Node.js. That is the benefit of Node.js; you can use one programming language in the frontend and the backend. Other popular languages for backend development are Java, C#, Python, and PHP. All these languages also have good backend frameworks you can use.

Some frontend libraries and frameworks

In this book, we used React.js in the frontend, which is currently a popular option, but there are many other options that are also good, such as Angular and Vue.js.

Databases

You should also know how to use databases with your backend programming language. The database can be either an SQL or a NoSQL database, and it is good to know both options. You should also know how performance can be optimized with the database you are using and the queries you are executing.

Version control

Version control is something that you can't live without. Nowadays, Git is a really popular version control system and it's really important to know how to use it. It is also worthwhile to be familiar with repository management services, such as GitHub and GitLab.

Useful tools

There are also many different tools that can help to make your development process more efficient. Here, we are just mentioning a number of tools that might be useful for you. Gulp.js is an open source JavaScript toolkit to automate your tasks in the development process. Grunt is similar to the JavaScript task runner, which you can use to automate your process. Webpack is a JavaScript module bundler that creates static assets from your dependencies. The `create-react-app`, which we used in the previous chapters, actually uses Webpack under the hood.

Security

You have to know the basics of web security and how to handle these issues in web development. A good way to start learning is to read the *OWASP Top 10 Most Critical Web Application Security Risks* (`https://www.owasp.org/index.php/Category:OWASP_Top_Ten_Project`). Then, you have to learn how to handle these issues with the frameworks you are using.

Best practices

Software development always involves teamwork, and therefore, it is really important that everyone in a team is using common best practices. Here, we will go through some basic things that you have to take into account. This is not the whole list, but we will try to concentrate on some basic things that you should know.

Coding conventions

Coding conventions are guidelines that describe how the code should be written in a specific programming language. It makes the code more readable and easier to maintain. Naming conventions define how variables, methods, and more should be named. Naming is really important, because that helps developers understand the purpose of a certain unit in the program. The layout convention defines how the structure of the source code should look; for example, indenting and the use of spaces. The commenting convention defines how the source code should be commented on. Quite often, it is good to use some standardized ways of commenting, such as Javadoc with Java.

Most of the software development environments and editors offer tools that help you with code conventions. You can also use code formatters, such as Prettier for JavaScript.

Choosing the proper tools

You should always choose the proper tools that best fit your software development process. This makes your process more efficient and also helps you in the development life cycle. There are many tools to automate tasks in the development process, and it is a good way of avoiding mistakes that occur in repetitive tasks. Of course, the tools you use will depend on the process and the technologies you're using.

Choosing the proper technologies

When starting to develop an application, one of the first things to decide is which technologies (programming language, frameworks, databases, and so on) you should use. Quite often, it feels safe to select technologies that you have always used, but that's not always the optimal choice. The application itself normally imposes a number of limitations in relation to the technologies that you can use. For example, if you have to create a mobile application, there are several technologies that you can use; but if you have to develop a similar application that you have made many times, it might be wiser to use technologies that you are already very familiar with.

Minimizing the amount of coding

A common good practice is to minimize the amount of coding. This is really sensible because it makes code maintenance and testing much easier. **DRY** (short for **Don't Repeat Yourself**) is a common principle in software development. The basic idea of DRY is to reduce the amount of code by avoiding repetition in the code. It is always a good practice to split your source code into smaller components because smaller units are always easier to manage. Of course, the optimal structure depends on the programming language you are using. One good statement is also **Keep it Simple, Stupid (KISS)**, which should guide you in the right direction.

Summary

In this chapter, we covered the technologies that you should be familiar with if you want to become a full stack developer. The amount of knowledge that you should have might sound like a lot, but you don't have to be the master of all the technologies that we described. It is also good to understand some best practices of software development, because then, you can avoid common mistakes and your source code will be more readable and easier to maintain.

Questions

1. Why are coding conventions important?
2. Why should you try to avoid excessive coding?
3. Why are naming conventions important?

Further reading

Packt has other great resources available for learning about full stack development. These are as follows:

- *The Complete JavaScript Developer: A Primer to Full Stack JS* [Video], by Full Stack Training Ltd (`https://www.packtpub.com/application-development/complete-javascript-developer-primer-full-stack-js-video`)
- *Full Stack Development with JHipster*, by Deepu K Sasidharan, and Sendil Kumar N (`https://www.packtpub.com/application-development/full-stack-development-jhipster`)
- *Fundamentals of Continuous Delivery Pipeline* [Video], by Rafał Leszko (`https://www.packtpub.com/networking-and-servers/fundamentals-continuous-delivery-pipeline-video`)

Assessments

Chapter 1

1. Spring Boot is a Java-based web application framework that is based on Spring. With Spring Boot, you can develop standalone web applications with embedded application servers.
2. Eclipse is an open source **integrated development environment (IDE)**, and it is mostly used for Java programming, but it supports multiple other programming languages as well.
3. Maven is an open source software project-management tool. Maven can manage builds, documentation, testing, and more in the software development project.
4. The easiest way to start a new Spring Boot project is to create it with the Spring Initializr web page. This creates a skeleton for your project with the modules that you need.
5. If you are using the Eclipse IDE, you just activate your main class and press the **Run** button. You can also use the `mvn spring-boot:run` Maven command to run an application.
6. The Spring Boot starter package provides logging features for you. You can define the level of logging in the `application.properties` settings file.
7. The error and log messages can be seen in the Eclipse IDE console after you run the application.

Chapter 2

1. **Depenency Injection (DI)** is software development technology that helps the interaction between the classes, but at the same time keeps the classes independent.
2. The easiest way to utilize DI in Spring Boot is to use `@Autowired` annotation.

Chapter 3

1. **Object-relational mapping (ORM)** is a technique that allows you to fetch and manipulate data from a database using an object-oriented programming paradigm. **Java Persistence API (JPA)** provides object-relational mapping for Java developers. Hibernate is a Java-based JPA implementation.

2. The entity class is just a standard Java class that is annotated with the `@Entity` annotation. You have to implement constructors, fields, getters, and setters inside the class. The unique ID field(s) are annotated with the `@Id` annotation.

3. You have to create a new interface that extends the Spring Data `CrudRepository` interface. You define the entity and the type of the `id` field in the type arguments—for example, `<Car, Long>`.

4. `CrudRepository` provides all CRUD operations to your entity. You can create, read, update, and delete your entities using `CrudRepository`.

5. You have to create entity classes and link the entities using the `@OneToMany` and `@ManyToOne` annotations.

6. You can add demo data to your main application class using `CommandLineRunner`.

7. Define the endpoint for the H2 console in your `application.properties` file and enable it. Then, you can access the H2 console by navigating to the defined endpoint with a web browser.

8. You have to add the MariaDB dependency to the `pom.xml` file and define the database connection settings in the `application.properties` file. Remove the H2 database dependency from the `pom.xml` file if you have used that.

Chapter 4

1. REST is an architectural style for creating web services, and it defines a set of constraints.

2. The easiest way to create a RESTful web service with Spring Boot is to use the Spring Data REST starter package. By default, the Spring Data REST package finds all public repositories and creates automatically RESTful web services for your entities.

3. You can send a `GET` request to the endpoint of the entity. For example, if you have an entity class called `Car`, the Spring Data REST package creates an endpoint called `/cars` that can be used to fetch all cars.

4. You can send a `DELETE` request to the endpoint of the individual entity item. For example, `/cars/1` deletes a car with the ID `1`.

5. You can send a `POST` request to the endpoint of the entity. The header must contain the `Content-Type` field with the `application/json` value. The new item will be embedded in the request body.

6. You can send a `PATCH` request to the endpoint of the entity. The header must contain the `Content-Type` field with the `application/json` value. The updated item will be embedded in the request body.

7. You have to annotate your repository using the `@RepositoryRestResource` annotation. The query parameters are annotated using the `@Param` annotation.

Chapter 5

1. Spring Security provides security services for Java-based web applications.

2. You have to add the Spring Security starter package dependency to your `pom.xml` file. You can configure Spring Security by creating a security configuration class.

3. **JSON Web Token (JWT)** is a compact way to implement authentication in modern web applications. The size of the token is small, and so it can be sent in the URL, either in the `POST` parameter or inside the header.

4. You can use the Java JWT library, that is, the JWT library for Java. The authentication service class adds and reads the token. The filter classes handle the login and authentication process.

5. You have to add the Spring Boot test starter package to your `pom.xml` file. The Spring Boot test starter package provides a lot of nice testing utilities—for example, JUnit, AssertJ, and Mockito. When using the JUnit, the basic test classes are annotated with the `@SpringBootTest` annotation, and the test methods should start with the `@Test` annotation.

6. The test cases can be easily executed with the Eclipse IDE by running the test classes (**Run** | **JUnit test**). The test results can be seen in the **JUnit** tab.

Chapter 6

1. Node.js is an open source, JavaScript-based, server-side environment. Npm is a package manager for JavaScript.

2. You can find the installation packages and instructions for installing these on multiple operating systems at `https://nodejs.org/en/download`.

3. **Visual Studio Code (VS Code)** is an open source code editor for multiple programming languages.
4. You can find the installation packages and instructions for installing this on multiple operating systems at `https://code.visualstudio.com`.
5. You can create an app using the `npx create-react-app projectname` command.
6. You can run the app using the `npm start` or `yarn start` command.
7. You can start by modifying the `App.js` file, and when you save the modification, you will see the changes immediately in the web browser.

Chapter 7

1. Components are the basic building blocks of React apps. The React component can be created using a JavaScript function or the ES6 class.
2. The props and state are the input data for rendering the component. They are JavaScript objects, and the component is rerendered when the props or state change.
3. The data flow goes from the parent component to the child.
4. The components that only have props are called stateless components. The components that have both props and a state are called stateful components.
5. JSX is the syntax extension for JavaScript, and it is recommended that you use it with React.
6. The component life cycle methods are executed at certain phases of the component's life cycle.
7. Handling events in React is similar to handling DOM element events. The difference in React is that event naming uses the camelCase naming convention—for example, `onClick` or `onSubmit`.
8. We will often want to invoke a JavaScript function that has access to form data after the form submission. Therefore, we have to disable the default behavior using the `preventDefault()` function. You can use the input field's `onChange` event handler to save the values from the input field to the state.

Chapter 8

1. A promise is an object that represents the result of an asynchronous operation. The use of promises simplifies the code when performing asynchronous calls.
2. The `fetch` API provides the `fetch()`, which method that you can use to make asynchronous calls using JavaScript.
3. When using the REST API, it is recommended that you use the `fetch()` call inside the `componentDidMount()` life cycle method that is invoked when the component has been mounted.
4. You can access the response data using the promises with the `fetch()` method. The data from the response is saved to the state and the component is rerendered when the state changes.

Chapter 9

1. You can download React components from multiple sources—for example, `https://js.coach/` or `https://github.com/brillout/awesome-react-components`.
2. You can install React components using the `npm` or `yarn` package managers. If you are using `npm`, use the `npm install <componentname>` command.
3. You have to install the `ReactTable` component. After the installation, you can use the `ReactTable` component in the `render()` method. You have to define the data and the columns using the `ReactTable` props. The data can be an object or an array.
4. You have to install the Material-UI component library using the `npm install @material-ui/core` command. After the library is installed, you can start to use the components. The documentation of the different components can be found at `https://material-ui.com`.
5. Routing can be implemented using the React Router component, which can be found at `https://github.com/ReactTraining/react-router`.

Chapter 10

1. With the mock up, it is much easier to discuss the needs with the client before you start to write any actual code. Changes to the mock up are really easy and quick to make, compared to modifications with real frontend source code.

2. You can modify the security configuration class to allow access to all endpoints without authentication.

Chapter 11

1. First, you have to call the REST API using the `fetch()` method. Then, you can access the response data using the promises with the `fetch()` method. The data from the response is saved to the state and the component is rerendered when the state changes.

2. You have to send a `DELETE` method request using the `fetch()` method. The endpoint of the call is the link to the item that you want to delete.

3. You have to send a `POST` method request to the entity endpoint using the `fetch()` method. The added item should be embedded in the body. You have to add the `Content-Type` header with the `application/json` value.

4. You have to send a `PATCH` method request using the `fetch()` method. The endpoint of the call is the link to the item that you want to update. The updated item should be embedded in the body. You have to add the `Content-Type` header with the `application/json` value.

5. You can use a third-party React component, such as React Toastify, to show toast messages.

6. You can use a third-party React component, such as React CSV, to export data to a CSV file.

Chapter 12

1. Material-UI is the component library for React, and it implements Google's material design.

2. First, you have to install the Material-UI library using the `npm install @material-ui/core` command. Then, you can start to use components from the library. The documentation of the different components can be found at `https://material-ui.com/`.

3. You can remove a component using the npm command npm remove
   <componentname>.

Chapter 13

1. Jest is a test library for JavaScript developed by Facebook.
2. Create a test file using the .test.js extension. Implement your test cases inside
   the file. You can run the tests using the npm test command.
3. For snapshot testing, you have to install the react-test-render package and
   import renderer to your test file. Implement your snapshot test cases inside the
   file and run the tests using the npm test command.
4. Enzyme is a JavaScript library for testing the React component's output.
5. Using the following npm command, npm install enzyme enzyme-adapter-
   react-16 --save-dev, we can install Enzyme.
6. You have to import the Enzyme and Adapter components to your test file. Then,
   you can create your test cases to render a component. With Enzyme, you can use
   Jest for assertions. Enzyme provides the simulate method that can be used to
   test events.

Chapter 14

1. You have to create a new component that renders input fields for the username
   and the password. The component also contains a button that calls the /login
   endpoint when the button is pressed.
2. The call from the login component is made using the POST method and a user
   object is embedded in the body. If the authentication succeeds, the backend sends
   the token back in the Authorization header.
3. The token can be saved to session storage using the
   sessionStorage.setItem() method.
4. The token has to be included in the request's Authorization header.

Chapter 15

1. You can create an executable JAR file by using the `mvn clean install` Maven command.
2. The easiest way to deploy a Spring Boot application is to push your application source code to GitHub and use the GitHub link from Heroku.
3. The easiest way to deploy the React app to Heroku is to use the Heroku Buildpack for `create-react-app`, which can be found at `https://github.com/mars/create-react-app-buildpack`.
4. Docker is a container platform that makes software development, deployment, and shipping easier. Containers are lightweight and executable software packages that include everything that is needed to run software.
5. The Spring Boot application is just an executable JAR file that can be executed with Java. You can use it to create a Docker container for your Spring Boot application in a similar way to creating one for any Java JAR application.
6. You can pull the latest MariaDB container from the Docker Hub using the `docker pull mariadb:latest` Docker command.

Chapter 16

1. It makes code more readable and easier to maintain. It also makes teamwork much easier because everyone is using the same structure in the coding.
2. It makes code more readable and easier to maintain. The testing of the code is easier.
3. It makes code more readable and easier to maintain. It also makes teamwork much easier because everyone is using the same naming convention in the coding.

Other Books You May Enjoy

If you enjoyed this book, you may be interested in these other books by Packt:

Spring Boot 2 Fundamentals
Patrick Cornelißen

ISBN: 9781789804980

- Create your own Spring Boot application from scratch
- Write comprehensive unit tests for your applications
- Store data in a relational database
- Build your own RESTful API with Spring Boot
- Developa rich web interface for your applications
- Secure your application with Spring Security

Spring 5.0 Projects
Nilang Patel

ISBN: 9781788390415

- Build Spring based application using Bootstrap template and JQuery
- Understand the Spring WebFlux framework and how it uses Reactor library
- Interact with Elasticsearch for indexing, querying, and aggregating data
- Create a simple monolithic application using JHipster
- Use Spring Security and Spring Security LDAP and OAuth libraries for Authentication
- Develop a microservice-based application with Spring Cloud and Netflix
- Work on Spring Framework with Kotlin

Leave a review - let other readers know what you think

Please share your thoughts on this book with others by leaving a review on the site that you bought it from. If you purchased the book from Amazon, please leave us an honest review on this book's Amazon page. This is vital so that other potential readers can see and use your unbiased opinion to make purchasing decisions, we can understand what our customers think about our products, and our authors can see your feedback on the title that they have worked with Packt to create. It will only take a few minutes of your time, but is valuable to other potential customers, our authors, and Packt. Thank you!

Index

Made in the USA
Las Vegas, NV
26 April 2021